FOOTSTEPS OF THE CELTS
BY RAIL

FOOTSTEPS OF THE CELTS BY RAIL

William Bleasdale

Book Guild Publishing
Sussex, England

First published in Great Britain in 2009 by
The Book Guild Ltd
Pavilion View
19 New Road
Brighton, BN1 1UF

Typesetting in Garamond by
Keyboard Services, Luton, Bedfordshire

Printed and bound in Thailand under the supervision of
MRM Graphics Ltd, Winslow, Bucks

A catalogue record for this book is available from
The British Library

ISBN 978 1 84624 352 3

To John and Robin

Contents

1

Ireland 2007

The myths, legends and turbulent history of Ireland make it a fascinating place and this, together with its beautiful countryside and the many historical sites, should make it a must on people's list of places to visit.

As far as I know I don't have any Irish ancestors but every time I get off the boat I get a definite feeling of belonging. Despite visiting many times, I have never used the rail network and this journey, for me, is long overdue. Although several branch lines have been closed and the narrow gauge system decimated, it is still possible to cover the majority of the Republic by rail.

It is a beautiful hot morning and the first part of the journey is a comfortable and smooth train ride along the North Wales coast to catch the afternoon ferry from Dun Laoghaire. The sea glints in the sunlight as the line skirts the coast until we approach Bangor where there are thick banks of foxgloves in full flower on either side of the line until suddenly the train plunges into the long tunnel that leads to Bangor station.

From here to the Menai Straits is a short distance but the view is beautiful as the train at this point is high above the water and I can see small boats dotted about on the water far below between Telford's 1826 suspension bridge and Stephenson's Britannia rail bridge of 1850.

Because of difficulties with the Admiralty, Stephenson had to change his original idea of two 350-foot cast iron arches over the Menai Straits and the final decision was then to use rectangular iron tubes mounted on perpendicular stone supports. The tubes were assembled ashore, floated into position on pontoons, and then hydraulically raised to the proper level.

The foundation stone was laid by Mr Frank Forster, the resident engineer, on 10th April 1846 and the bridge was opened to single line traffic on 18th March 1850, the second line being opened on 19th October 1850.

To complete this remarkable feat of design and engineering the famous Egyptian Lions, carved from limestone, were placed at each entrance to the bridge. These were the work of the sculptor John Thomas, who was born in 1813 at Chelford, Gloucestershire, of Welsh ancestry.

The single-track bridge of today is quite different from the one that stood here until the night of Saturday May 23rd 1970 when two young juveniles caused it to catch fire, a blaze that lasted for nine hours. The accumulated oil and tar of many years caused a fire so fierce that the metal of the tubes became white hot and reduced the tubular structure to a mass of twisted metal; the twin girder arches that now support the railway and the road above it were finally completed in 1980 although railway service had been restored long before then.

One benefit since the fire is that you now have a grandstand view from the train of the Menai Straits far below as you cross over them.

We have just passed Gaerwen and although they have been severed from the main line I can just see the lines of the Amlwch branch disappearing into the undergrowth. There is some interest in reopening this line but it will take a lot of money and enthusiasm.

The sea terminal at Holyhead is a bit spartan but it is modern, clean and there are good cafe and tourist information facilities. I fall into a long conversation with a young man called Andy who has just got off the boat from Ireland.

The crossing takes about an hour and a half but after about an hour there is a tremendous bang and the ship shudders as though it has hit something. The engines are reduced in power for a short while and then resume their normal speed. Passengers are left to wonder whether we will reach Dun Laoghaire.

I am impressed at Dun Laoghaire not only by the clean and modern facilities, compared to when I last came, but also at finding my case already on the carousel when I arrive. Outside I can see the extensive marina and there are so many yachts and boats that you can hardly see the water.

The plan had been for us to travel by coach to Connolly station and from there by the new light rail system (LUAS) in Dublin centre to Heuston station. It is 5.30 pm and there is considerable doubt about getting through the tremendous rush hour in Dublin city centre, so we are going to make a detour in the coach of about three miles, direct to the station. It still takes about 90 minutes through the tremendous traffic that moves in and around Dublin, and we arrive for the train with about ten minutes to spare.

For anyone travelling into and around Dublin from Dun Laoghaire I recommend the DART and LUAS every time. The Dublin Area Rapid Transit (DART) is part of the suburban railway system that runs along the east coast between Howth in County Dublin and Greystones in County Wicklow.

Heuston station is a very imposing building and when it was commissioned in 1844 it was based on the design of an Italian palazzo. The station building is a block of nine bays with Corinthian columns and balustrades and there are carved swags and urns. Despite its somewhat square appearance it is nevertheless a very attractive and impressive building and when it was opened in 1846 it was the largest enclosed structure on earth.

The station is on Dublin South Quay, upriver from the Guinness brewery in James Street. The nearby iron bridge that spans the River Liffey was

Heuston Station

built to commemorate the visit of King George IV in 1821 and was completed in 1827. When the Great Southern & Western Railway (GS&WR) terminus opened at Heuston in 1846 it was known as Kingsbridge station. It was renamed in 1966, after Sean Heuston, an Easter Rising leader who had worked in the station offices. Heuston serves all the main towns and cities of Ireland except Sligo, Rosslare and the line to Belfast; these all start from Connolly station.

There is just ten minutes to catch the 19.05 to Athlone and as I sink back in the comfort of the inter-city carriage after fighting through all that Dublin traffic, I suddenly feel very relaxed – but train travel always has that effect on me.

Just a few minutes later and we are passing Inchicore where Ireland's largest railway works are situated, and which was once the citadel of GS&WR and CIE (Coras Iompair Eireann, the national authority for public transport in Eire) steam.

We have passed through Kildare which is the limit of the commuter service from Dublin and I can now see the Curragh racecourse with its own part-time station. It is a common sight to see horses being exercised while sheep graze placidly nearby. A little to the south of Kildare is the Irish National Stud which I will be visiting in a few days' time.

Sharing my carriage is a group of about 15 school children aged between ten and eleven; they have been enjoying a cultural visit to Dublin for the day and their teachers Rosalin and Deidre tell me that they have been on the go since six o'clock that morning. The children, although well behaved, are very noisy and don't show any sign of tiredness. I have a long discussion with the two teachers about special education needs, kids today, safety and all sorts of other things and it is very interesting to share opinions and thoughts on so many things. I can't help admiring their stamina in looking after this very energetic bunch of children for the last 15 hours. Rosalin and Deidre say that they will remember me as William with George the cat (I told them that I live on my own with a big tabby called George).

On the way to Ballinasloe

Deidre and Rosalin

We have just passed Portalington and the line has divided and become single track to Athlone, but continues as double track on the main line to Cork.

I arrive at Athlone at 9.10 pm and transfer to the very comfortable Creggan Court Hotel just outside the town. I am having an early night tonight as tomorrow will be a long day including a train journey to Galway followed by a coach tour through the Connemara National Park to Westport and then another train journey from there back to Athlone.

I am up at 6.00 am and after a leisurely breakfast there is time to explore Athlone; this town is the geographical centre of Ireland. Although it is very warm there is a pleasant tree-lined walkway interspersed with beds of yellow and white roses by the side of the Shannon River, and the breeze from the water makes it a very pleasant stroll. Under the trees there is a statue of John McCormack, a world-famous tenor who was born in Athlone in 1884 and died in Dublin in 1946.

As I turn and cross the river on the lovely old stone bridge I can see the town's thirteenth-century castle which still survives although it is now dominated by the Church of St Peter and St Paul across the road. Because of its strategic location near the centre of the town the castle was central to the siege of Athlone in 1691.

Upstream I can see the white-painted iron girders of the railway bridge and between there and where I am standing there are a lot of motor cruisers moored in a little marina. A man is sitting in the stern of one of the boats idly throwing bread to several ducks until suddenly, as if by magic, there are ducks everywhere.

Athlone Castle   The Shannon at Athlone

A cruiser edges out from its mooring and the ducks bob in its wake. The water slowly drifts under the road bridge until it cascades over the weir further down. Near to the weir I can see a replica Viking boat which takes visitors and tourists on a cruise along the River Shannon to Lough Ree where Viking invaders once pillaged and plundered the many islands in the area.

The name 'Athlone' comes from two Irish words, 'Ath' meaning 'ford' and 'Luain', a man's name – 'the ford of Luain'. The town's historical importance was due to its position by a natural ford in the River Shannon.

Athlone is situated at the very edge of County Westmeath and although I will not have an opportunity during this brief visit to see them, there are many interesting things to see in this county such as: the Seven Wonders of Fore, which include the water that flows uphill, the water that won't boil and the tree that won't burn; Lough Derrvaragh and the Children of Lir; the Gothic Tullynally Castle; Locke's Distillery in Kilbeggan, the 'oldest licensed distillery in the world' (according to the local tourist information), established in 1757; and the interesting town of Mullingar with its association with James Joyce and *Ulysses*.

Athlone today is a busy and prosperous town and is also the point at which the railway line from Dublin divides and goes either to Westport/Ballina or Galway. There used to be another railway line from Athlone to Mullingar on the Dublin to Sligo line but that was closed some years ago. I have already discovered that although this line and several others have been closed it appears to be the policy of Irish Rail to leave the rails in situ following closure and indeed the line to Mullingar, together with some others, now appear to be likely candidates to reopen in the not too distant future. This would not only make a very convenient link for passengers between the Galway and Sligo lines, obviating the need for them to return to Dublin to travel to the west, but would also enable Irish Rail to run trains to Galway and Westport from Connolly station as well as Heuston.

The original station in Athlone used to be at the end of the white girder bridge but a new combined rail and bus station was built nearer the town centre and opened in 1985. The old station is now used as offices but its closed doors and boarded up ground-floor windows make it a somewhat forbidding-looking place.

Across from the bridge is the main street of this pleasant town which is what I would call typical in that it is rather narrow but has lots of varied and interesting shops. Although it is still only 9.30 in the morning there are a lot of people about and the bridge is busy with traffic.

It is time to head for the station and the 10.48 train to Galway. Inside the booking hall there is a brass plaque with the names of all 34 stationmasters that there have been at Athlone since it originally opened. Outside there is a woman sitting knitting on the platform while she waits for her train; despite the speed of her needles she manages to give her full attention to the man next to her who she is having a conversation with. The train is on time and is efficiently greeted and despatched by the station staff.

Athlone station

Railway bridge over the Shannon

I have already noticed what a smooth and comfortable ride the trains are and I think that it must be a combination of the wider 5 foot 3 inch gauge coupled with the upgraded track. Both here and for the next ten days, I notice signs at all the stations advertising the involvement of the European Union in funding the upgrading of all the lines and refurbishment of all the stations. In terms of comfort and numbers of passengers it appears to have been a good investment.

The Galway train at Athlone   St Peter and St Pauls Church, Athlone

Very shortly we reach the white girder bridge over the Shannon and our progress over it is very slow due to maintenance work. Immediately after the bridge is the old station that I have already referred to.

Almost immediately we are running through beautiful green countryside – everything in Ireland is very green; well, not quite everything as we are just passing a field that is a blaze of yellow buttercups. Suddenly, there is the wonderful sight of a young grey foal with a black tail staggering about near his mother. He is obviously not long born and he is a joy to watch.

The view of the flat landscape here is always changing from banks of gorse bushes to peat fields and then lots of trees. There is a small farm surrounded by forestry, but otherwise there is no sign of habitation as far as the eye can see.

A heron takes off from a small pond, his large wings lazily lifting him off before he glides gracefully away. A brand new cottage appears out of nowhere; it is painted a brilliantly bright yellow. I was to discover later that nearly all the new cottages are painted in some bright colour: I didn't make a note but in one place I saw one painted the most vivid scarlet that I have ever seen.

This locomotive is hauling five coaches but the intention of Irish Rail is to have all lines served by multiple units with the exception of the Dublin to Cork express route.

We have just passed a lovely old red brick station; it seems little changed from when it was built and it still has its water tower for steam trains. There are a lot of country level crossings on this line and the locomotive's horn blares almost continually.

Galway station is a fairly bleak barn of a place with just two lines in and one platform, and the whole place is devoid of interest but is very clean and tidy. The first news to greet me on the platform is to not drink the tap water, as the local lough has been polluted.

The station is named after Eamonn Ceannt, who was a patriot from the 1916 Easter Rising. It is behind what was the Great Southern Hotel, a majestic reminder of Ireland's great railway days, now called the Hotel Meyrick. The change of name does not seem to have detracted from its quality, as inside, despite some refurbishment work in progress, it is very luxurious.

In front of the hotel is Eyre Square, a very busy place. Dotted about the central green area are paths and modern sculptures. There is also a sculpture of a Galway hooker, a traditional wooden sailing boat with a broad black hull, a thick mast and brown sails; these boats used to sail up and down the Atlantic coast carrying peat and cattle. It is very hot and there are a lot of people about, some of whom are seeking the shade of the several trees that are about; an ice cream seller is doing a roaring trade.

Galway is the centre for the Irish-speaking regions in the west and is also a university city. I remember it as a very compact town and easy to explore, and decide to walk down to the harbour on my left and follow the headland round to the river estuary and back through the bustle of the main shopping and eating part of the town. The Arran Doolin ferry is in and there are also several trawlers and yachts. This is the Commercial Dock and it is much like small docks everywhere. There is a red brick building with 'The Limerick Steamship Co. Ltd.' engraved in the stonework but it now appears to be an estate agent's premises.

As I follow the headland round from the harbour past the old dock, it is suddenly peaceful and there are very few people about. As I stroll along the grass-topped banks I can look towards Galway Bay. Although it will not be possible this time, I have seen the sun go down on Galway Bay.

I am now at what is both an inner harbour and the point where the River Corrib starts to widen out before it reaches Galway Bay. With the tide out and the fresh water of the river washing through the sand and stones there are plenty of feeding opportunities for the 200 or so swans that I can see. On the other side of the river used to be The Claddagh, an independent fishing community beyond the original city walls. This community was governed by a 'King' until the last one died in 1954. It seems that the only reminder of this Gaelic-speaking community are Claddagh betrothal rings which were traditionally handed down from mother to daughter, and the road on the other side from me which is called Claddagh Quay.

On the grass-topped harbour wall I can see a young girl of about 20 sitting with her legs tucked under her. She is playing a guitar and singing softly to herself and every so often she makes a note in a book in front of her; it is a very tranquil scene.

Emily in Galway

I ask if I can talk with her and she tells me that her name is Emily and she is from New York and is here in Galway until August. She says that she loves Ireland and its people and spends a lot of her time singing and playing in pubs here and will be sorry when she has to return home. Today she is learning a new song, and what I thought was a notebook is actually a book of music. Her parents are from New York but her grandmother originally came from Cork and emigrated to America many years ago. She talks with great fondness of her grandmother and then asks me why I am in Ireland, when I explain that it is about seeing as much of Ireland as I can via the rail system and that I hope for it to be part of a book about foreign rail travel, she expresses great interest and promises to buy *Rails over the Andes* when she returns to America.

Just after leaving Emily I walk through the Spanish Arch. This is one of four that were built in 1584 to protect the harbour, which was outside the city walls at that time and where the Spanish traders unloaded their cargoes. It is a very thick wall and as I walk through the arch I have to stoop slightly. A man walks past dressed in a canary-coloured shirt, white jacket, black trousers and bright yellow shoes – a very striking picture.

I have now entered one of the narrow streets leading to Eyre Square and there are lots of shops and cafes with tables and chairs outside. Galway has thrived in recent years and is now a vibrant and busy city, popular

Galway

with visitors and students alike, all of which gives it a very cosmopolitan air.

In Easons bookshop I try to buy a book on Irish railways and although Sinnead, the assistant, is very helpful she cannot find anything on her computer; that surprises me a bit. We have a discussion on train travel and she thinks that my five-day Irish Rover ticket for 138 euros is a bargain. She says that many people travel to Dublin from Galway although the train fare is twice that of the bus, but the train is still popular because it takes half the time that the bus does.

All the little shops are very colourful with interesting names such as Twice as Nice, and there are some very interesting and old pubs such as The Quays, The Slate House and Ti Neachtain, which used to be a town house belonging to 'Humanity Dick' a nineteenth-century MP who introduced laws against cruelty to animals, and was considered to be a founder of the RSPCA.

On a corner near William Street there are two bronze statues one of which depicts Oscar Wilde. In-between these statues are two young women entertaining the crowds with very catchy Irish music played on a fiddle and a flute; they are really putting their hearts into it.

Galway

Music in Galway

The Spanish Arch

Back in Eyre Square I relax under a tree for a few minutes before the next leg of the journey, which is a coach trip through the Connemara National Park to Westport where there will be a train back to Athlone.

Heading west along the shores of Lough Corrib we pass through a small town called Moycullen, and further on at Maam Cross we turn and head north towards Leenaun. We are now in Joyce country and the Maumturk Mountains which are all around us remind me very much of Snowdonia. It is now raining in earnest.

Forty-two miles from Galway and we have arrived in Leenaun. It has stopped raining but the sky is grey and it is oppressively warm. It is a pretty little place and nestles in a valley between the mountains at the head of The Killary, which is Ireland's only fjord. From here the sea is 5 miles away.

There are a few shops, a pub and a sheep and wool museum. Outside the pub there are two men having an argument about some obscure subject that I couldn't discover; they are happy for me to sit with them but are

The Killary – Ireland's only fjord

too absorbed in their argument to take much notice of me and my questions. One of the men comes from County Mayo and the other appears to gain the advantage when he says that he is a Roscommon man and therefore intellectually superior to his companion. His companion has obviously been patronising the pub for quite some time and is very much the worst for wear although it is a close thing as to who has had the most to drink. For all their intensity there is no suggestion that the situation might become physical.

Inside the pub all is peaceful. It has a very traditional air and there are many posters and pictures about *The Field*, a film that was made in this area, starring Richard Harris. I have ordered a pint of Guinness and a cheese and onion sandwich. The Guinness is perfection and I wonder again why I cannot find Guinness like this back home. The sandwich is two slices of bread with cheese and onion in-between, but there the simplicity ends because there is so much of it that I see myself spending the afternoon here just trying to eat it. Still, it is an excellent reason to have a second pint of Guinness.

Sitting on the little bridge outside, listening to the River Erriff gurgling over the stones on its way to the fjord, I reflect what an unspoilt and peaceful place this is, and it is a shame to leave.

After Leenaun the journey continues through the majestic surroundings of the Partry Mountains with their Loughs and rivers, until just before we reach Westport we pass Croagh Patrick (known locally as 'The Reek') on the left. This is Ireland's holy mountain, named after St Patrick, and is where it is said he spent 40 days fasting and praying for the Irish. It is also the place at which he cast out all the reptiles of Ireland.

The tree-lined road leading to the town centre of Westport is very attractive and there is a river running alongside with a fountain in the middle. The water suddenly tumbles over a little weir and under a very old stone bridge. Everywhere there are hanging baskets of very colourful flowers, even hanging from the bridge.

The place has charm and character and is well known for traditional music; there is also an arts festival every September. It was also the winner in 2001 and 2006 of the title 'Ireland's Tidiest Town'.

Unfortunately there will be no time to explore Westport because of the waiting train but I do notice that it is extremely hilly, which surprises me as the town is so close to the sea. The station is quite a way out of town and is both quaint and modern and has been the winner of the best-kept station prize on several occasions. The spotlessly clean booking hall has a customer information book containing everything you need to know. The station somehow combines being modern, clean and efficient with a sort of homely and local feel about it.

Gardens at Westport station

Westport

The big locomotive with its eight carriages is ready to go, and tonight dinner will be on the train during the journey back to Athlone.

I am back in the hotel at 8.30 pm after a delightful dinner on the train of salmon and fresh vegetables followed by a sweet that melted in the mouth; the meal lasted for almost the full two hours of the journey. It has been a long day and I head for my room to complete my notes for the day and have an early night.

Thursday is another grey day but it is still very warm. Today is another train journey from Athlone; it will be a Westport train again but for me it will be only as far as Manulla Junction where there is a change to catch another train to Ballina. The interesting thing about Manulla Junction is that it can only be accessed by train.

There is a two-car unit waiting to take passengers on the final half-hour journey to Ballina and this is indeed a picturesque journey with many different sorts of trees, small loughs and mountains. Everything is very green and there are only isolated cottages here and there.

We are just running alongside Lough Cullin, with Lough Conn beyond it, and at the edge of the water I can see a heron, patiently waiting for his next meal.

I get into conversation with Teresa, who lives in Dublin. She has a daughter in Ballina and is visiting her for a week. She thinks the train service is excellent and says that it is very easy to get from Dublin to Ballina. She expresses herself quite forcefully on the subject of immigration into Ireland of non-Irish and I steer her into safer waters and tell her about some of my other train journeys: she is very interested in them and asks me many questions about South America.

We have just stopped at Foxford which is the only station on this section of line; it is a very sleepy sort of place with lots of ivy covering the outside walls of the waiting room. Foxford itself is a quiet market town with a population of about 1,000 and is a good base for the excellent angling on nearby Lough Conn. There are also the famous Foxford Woollen Mills which were founded by an Irish nun in 1892 and are still thriving today in conjunction with an interesting visitor centre.

Ballina station is quite pretty with lots of flowers, and although the street outside the station appears fairly uninteresting, we are some way from the centre of the town. Opposite the station is Paddy Jordan's Bar which looks very inviting but there is no time to find out as the schedule is a bit tight. The coach journey will allow some time in Sligo before the train to Dromod and the Cavan & Leitrim narrow gauge railway.

Heading north through Corbally the area is very flat and there is a lot forestry, but reaching Dromore West the view changes dramatically as on my left now is the rocky coast of Sligo Bay with Aughris Head thrusting out from the mainland. A little further on, across the estuary I can now see Carrowmore, where there is the largest group of megalithic monuments in Ireland and a huge Neolithic burial ground. Nearby Knocknarea Mountain dates back about 5,000 years and the cairn on the top is said to contain the tomb of Queen Maeve of Connaught.

Just before Sligo is a pretty village called Ballyisodare and here I can see a series of waterfalls with brown peaty water rushing and tumbling over them. The first building of note in Sligo is a large, grey and forbidding affair and it turns out to be the County Asylum although I wasn't able to find out whether it still had that role. The road curves round the harbour with a bridge over the river that flows from Lough Gill to the sea. The tide is out and there are many birds feeding among the rocks and seaweed.

It is time to explore this interesting town. Sligo lies between Lough Gill and the Atlantic and has an active arts scene and is known as the arts

Sligo

Sligo station

capital of north-west Ireland. It is also the birthplace of W.B. Yeats (1865–1939), the famous Irish poet who described his beloved Co. Sligo in his *Reveries over Childhood and Youth*. Yeats is buried in Drumcliffe churchyard just north of Sligo, and within sight of Ben Bulben ridge which is Sligo's most famous mountain that rises dramatically out of the surrounding plain and was made famous by Yeats in his writing. Yeats also composed his own epitaph and it is inscribed on the tall grey stone that marks his final resting place. It reads: 'Cast a cold eye on Life, on Death. Horseman pass by'.

Just in front of me is Hyde Bridge, this is a lovely old stone arched bridge that crosses the river. Today it is swollen by rain and rushes beneath, bursting over rocks on its way to the sea. Opposite me is O'Connell Street where the main shopping is, and it is interesting to stroll along here looking at the variety of things for sale in the many different shops. There are a lot of people and it is very busy. Back on the bridge is a large glass-fronted building, the Yeats Memorial Building which also houses the Sligo Art Gallery; there is also a restaurant which is full of people enjoying a meal while the river flows past them. Not far from here is the town's only surviving medieval building, Sligo Abbey; it is a well-preserved ruin and dates from 1252.

I realise that I have been dawdling and time is going quickly. I have yet another train to catch and I am not yet sure exactly where the station is! After wandering down Wine Street past a small modern shopping mall, I come across the station perched on a hill overlooking the town. It is an old station with the platform canopy long gone although the metal frame work is still there. In the booking hall there is a fascinating collection of old posters and photographs including one of repairing the station after

1916 Proclamation poster – Sligo station

the troubles. Waiting at the platform is a very modern and clean four-car diesel multiple unit that will take me on the next leg to Dromod; its green and yellow paintwork is spotless.

It is about an hour's run to Dromod and as we leave Sligo station I can see that the old turntable is still in place. The countryside around here is beautiful with lots of trees, everything is very green and the mountains brooding in the background. All the mountain peaks are marching in a row with a backdrop of grey clouds.

The first station is Collooney and it is just a modern halt, although the original building is still here but bricked up. Ballymote is next and here the gardens are very attractive and there are some lovely hanging baskets; unlike Collooney the original station building here is still in use. There is a very large ruined castle adjacent to the station.

The upgrade to all of Ireland's railways is very evident with refurbished stations and upgraded track; this train is really moving at the moment and it is a very smooth ride indeed, as all of them have been so far.

One thing that I have noticed is that generally between stations there is usually just miles of nothingness with the occasional house or farm; this is not to say that the countryside is not beautiful, just that generally human habitation seems to be very much concentrated around the towns.

Boyle station is almost a copy of Ballymote and there are now lots of horses in the fields. Carrick-on-Shannon station is yet another very attractive place with many flowers and hanging baskets. The other platform is planted with beautiful flowers and bright paintwork and is obviously very well looked after, but there are no rails on that side!

Between Carrick and Dromod the line follows the River Shannon for a while and the river gives the appearance of being almost man-made in the

Dromod narrow gauge station

way it runs in an organised way through the countryside with later on a regulated set of S-bends. As we run over a wide bridge across the Shannon, great beds of reeds are bowing before the wind. A little brook appears and it is a blaze of yellow kingcups.

Dromod: this is a station on the Dublin to Sligo line but is also home to the Cavan & Leitrim Railway which is based in the original narrow gauge station adjacent to the main line. The Cavan & Leitrim light railway company was incorporated in 1883. Its independent narrow gauge railway opened in 1888 over a 33-mile length between Dromod and Belturbet. It had nine locomotives and 167 other vehicles, and it eventually closed in 1959. Halfway along the line there was also a branch from Ballinamore to Arigna. The reason for the line surviving longer than some of its fellow narrow gauge lines was that at Arigna there was one of Ireland's very few coal deposits.

We are here to meet Mike who, with a handful of volunteers, is endeavouring to recreate as much as he can of the original line. Currently it runs for about half a mile to a temporary terminus at Clooncolry, and they hope to extend it for a further five miles across the moorland to Mohill.

Mike was described to me as the most Irish Irishman that you could find, and I understand the description when we meet. He has on a much-used dark red pullover with a locomotive driver's hat at a jaunty angle over one eye, and his whole appearance is that of a driver who has just finished his shift at the regulator. He talks quickly and with his very strong accent and irrepressible enthusiasm and humour you have to concentrate hard to

Mike

follow him. His eyes are full of humour and he is a lovely person to talk to.

First there is a short ride to the current terminus and back; this is in a Great Southern Railways inspection car from 1927 and it is in lovely condition. The locomotive is a little diesel shunter, as unfortunately his steam locomotive is out of action for the moment with boiler problems.

Back at the yard, Mike runs out from the shed a little War Department diesel locomotive from 1942 and tells us a bit about its history and how he acquired it. The other contents of the shed include a 1912 Guinness steam locomotive. Although that and the other items in here have undoubtedly seen better days, Mike croons over them like children and his enthusiasm and commitment are incredible.

Outside, and the best description of the area I can give, without wishing to be unkind in any way, is of a huge junk yard, but nevertheless an interesting junk yard. There is a large and bewildering array of items on display, most of them nothing to do with railways, and virtually all of them are in poor condition. Mike obviously views them with a less critical eye and gives a long and detailed description and history of many of the items. Most of the items also have a written description alongside them. I think that if there was enough money to engage on a restoration programme then it would indeed form the basis for an attractive transport museum.

There were far too many items for me to list and the following is a sample of what was on view. Several narrow gauge wagons from the original line. A 1950s railcar. Several 8-pounder field guns. A small steam locomotive built in Dublin in 1912. Original trespass signs from the Cavan & Leitrim Railway. Several single- and double-decker buses. Various lorries from the 1940s and 1950s. An RTE (Radio Telefis Eireann) television outside broadcast van. Several ambulances of 1950s vintage. An experimental Murphy miniature submarine built in the 1980s.

A propeller from a Luftwaffer Dornier number 18 flying boat found on the sea bed off County Wexford. A propeller from a Junkers 88. A 1950 Bristol single-decker bus used by Crosville in North Wales; its Crosville number was SOG 156. An old Mercedes breakdown truck. A Leitrim County Fire Service fire engine from many decades ago. A Cardinal hearse with the registration DIE 666, complete with coffin! A 1955 Percival Provost two-seater training aircraft. The front end of a Douglas DC7 long-range airliner. A Curtis radial engine, as used on a Douglas DC7C airliner. A Pratton Witney GT409 turbo jet engine. The cockpit of a 1961 Boeing 707 jet liner, and a 1959 Scammel Highwayman rail shunter that has been

Michael

DIE 666

Cavan & Leitrim

so attacked by rust that there are only thin strips of metal holding it together.

Outside the engine shed is the Cavan & Leitrim's main steam locomotive and it is a lovely picture with its red paint and gleaming brass dome. It was built by Kerr Stuart & Co. in 1916 and its number is 3024. Behind it is a little diesel shunter with the name *Dinmor* that was built by Fowler & Co. of Leeds in 1947 and today has obviously been used to shunt the Kerr loco into place. Both the locomotives are in front of the engine shed which, together with the water tower, are original to the line.

The station house and buildings are all original and are delightfully kept along with the neat gardens. Inside the booking office it is like a step back in time with all the original features in place, together with other items such as the station clock, which although not from Dromod is the same period as the station. The whole experience of the visit was very worthwhile.

After a good dinner last night of a seafood platter then Irish beef and Yorkshire pudding, followed by a good night's sleep, I am ready for another long day today which takes us by coach to Kilkee on the Atlantic coast for a one-night stay.

It's a bit breezy today and it is what you might call a 'lazy wind': it would rather go through you than round you. There is no main line train travel today but there are other treats such as the West Clare Railway towards the end of the day.

First stop is at Clonmacnoise. This was a monastic city founded by St Ciaran in 548 and is one of Ireland's most holy places. Many of the kings of Tara and Connaught are buried here and the Pope conducted a mass here in 1979; it is still a place of great pilgrimage. There are two round towers within the site, one of which is 1,000 years old, and from where I am standing, the fourteenth-century cathedral with its Whispering Arch is straight in front of me, but because of restoration work it is difficult to obtain worthwhile photographs.

Clonmacnoise is just a few miles south of Athlone and is situated on a small hill with the River Shannon at the bottom, and beyond that a broad

Ruins at Clonmacnoise

vista of green fields and trees with mountains in the far distance – it is a very peaceful place.

From here it is only a few minutes' drive to the small village of Shannonbridge and just beyond that is the Clonmacnoise & West Offaly Railway which is operated by the Irish Peat Board (Bord na Mona); the board was set up in 1946 to harvest peat for burning in electricity generating stations.

Driving through the entrance we are confronted by a lot of large sheds and railway tracks and it suddenly becomes obvious that this operation is conducted on a very large scale. At the entrance there is a monument to the peat cutters of the past.

The train ride is in a brightly painted yellow and green carriage hauled by a small diesel locomotive in the same livery, and is a 5-mile tour of the Blackwater Bog which covers 20,000 acres and stretches into four counties.

Monument to the peat cutters

As we move off we pass an open-air museum of the extraordinary-looking machines that used to cut the peat 50 years ago. There are a lot of them and they stand here like so many old monsters from some science fiction film. There is a guide who explains the history and development

The bog railway

Peat cutting

of the bog and how it turned from lakeland to marshy fen to bog. She also says that the peat here will be exhausted in 20 years' time and, after that, about 40 per cent of the total area will become a wildlife sanctuary with the rest being a mixture of grassland and forestry.

The power station, which is 125 megawatts, uses 800,000 tons of peat each year, or 40 train loads of peat a day. I make that 16 million tons of peat by the time this area ceases production, a staggering figure. Twelve per cent of Ireland's electricity is produced from peat-burning power stations.

As the peat is cut it is piled in very long pyramid-like lines where it dries, before being transported to the power station. A length of railway track is laid alongside the line of peat and when that has been moved the track is then lifted and relaid alongside the next row of peat.

Thirty feet below the surface of the bog are the remains of long-dead trees, such as oak, yew and birch, that were growing here between 5,000 and 7,000 years ago. During the peat cutting these dead trees are excavated and are put to one side to await treatment and 'restoration', when they become beautiful and decorative ornaments for the home and garden.

There is an area where peat extraction has finished and this has been turned into a wildlife sanctuary with small lakes and little islands and shows what the environment looked like 12,000 years ago. There are colourful flowers and some birds and one that I think is a sparrow, but later decide may have been a reed bunting.

As the train lurches along the track on a raised bank of earth we are surrounded by brown peat as far as the eye can see but when we make a stop to watch a demonstration of peat cutting by hand the ground is not just brown but a lovely mixture of rich brown and purple with different-coloured moss-like growths. I can also see a plant that has a very long stalk with white pyramid-like flowers on the top, it is very beautiful and is the bog orchid which is both rare and protected. It is incredibly quiet and peaceful here. A sudden brief glimpse of the sun reflects off the water of a small lake in the distance and for an instant there is a myriad of colour.

A final stop at the souvenir shop, where there are some very interesting and nice things to buy including items made with the bog wood; they seem expensive until I remember to convert the price from euros to pounds.

The Blackwater Bog has been a very interesting part of this journey and is far more than just the brown wasteland that I thought it might be, for with its wide range of flora and fauna, rich wildlife and peaceful beauty it is a fascinating place to visit.

We now turn west and through the one long street of Shannonbridge, and then across a lovely castellated stone bridge at the end; the bridge has many arches and there is an old fort at the far end which is now a restaurant. Immediately south of the bridge is the meeting point of counties Offaly, Galway and Roscommon, and also where the River Suck on its journey south from Lough O'Flynn joins the Shannon; we will be following the River Suck west but only as far as Ballinasloe, then we turn south to Loughrea and on to Ennis.

We are not stopping in Ballinasloe and have just passed an equestrian centre at the edge of town. As in most of Ireland, horses and horse racing are very popular. There is a traditional horse fair here every October which is one of the oldest in Europe, and it is attended by thousands of people over several days. The town also has a station on the Athlone to Galway line.

Loughrea ('town of the grey lake') sits next to the large lough that gives the town its name. On the top of nearby Monument Hill there is a megalithic tomb. Although it is not on the coast the town has a slight seaside air about it, as there is a huge grassed area in front of the lough almost like a promenade. There are a lot of new houses here and they are all colour-washed in different colours and look very attractive.

A lot of the fields around here are divided by stone walls — not the sort of layered stones that you associate with Yorkshire, but gigantic blocks instead; and why not if you have plenty of them?

We have reached Gort, about 18 miles from Ennis. This is a very old-fashioned Irish town with a big market centre and the place is busy today despite the rain that is now falling. Just north of the town is Coole, the former home of Lady Gregory who died in 1932. She was one of the founders of the famous Abbey Theatre in Dublin, and although her house no longer stands, there is the Autograph Tree in the grounds with the initials of George Bernard Shaw and W.B. Yeats carved into it.

Ennis is in County Clare and my first impression of it, with its manicured grass and lines of trees, is that it is a very neat and tidy town; it did in fact win the 'National Tidy Towns' award in 2005.

Just a short walk from the car park past the museum brings me to the junction of Abbey Street and O'Connell street, and reveals Ennis to be a charming but hectic little town. Here is a large monument to Daniel O'Connell with his statue on the top, built on the site of the Old Courthouse. The stone steps around its base are very convenient and there are a lot of young people sprawled over them; most of them seem to be talking on mobile phones. Nearby there is stall selling whelks and mussels.

Ennis

The inscription on the base of the monument reads: 'On this spot in the year 1828 Daniel O'Connell was returned M.P. proposed by O'Gorman Mahon, seconded by Tom Steele'. 'Honest Tom' Steele was a local farmer and friend of O'Connell.

Just round the corner is Gaol Street and down here is one of the many bookshops. Unfortunately I spend rather longer here than I should and this means I will have to hurry to see as much as I can of this very attractive and quaint town with its narrow and tortuous streets. In Market Place there is a market in full swing and one stall holder has rows and rows of pots with different-coloured roses in full bloom: lovely sight, lovely scents.

There are lots and lots of small and colourful shops and the whole town is bustling with people. Paddy Quinn's bar looks very tempting but I don't have time. Ennis dates from the thirteenth century and the narrow streets and old shops together with its air of charm help to maintain a medieval atmosphere.

In railway terms, Ennis today has lost a lot of its importance. It was formerly on the main line from Waterford and Limerick through to Athenry on the Dublin to Galway line, and then Claremorris on the Dublin to Westport and Ballina lines. It was also the starting point of the narrow gauge West Clare Railway that ran from Ennis through Miltown Malbay to Moyasta Junction, where trains then went either to Kilkee on the Atlantic coast of County Clare, or Kilrush on the edge of the Shannon estuary. Today, Ennis is now just a terminus for trains from Limerick, but there is a possibility that Irish Rail will, in the not too distant future, reopen the section from Ennis north through Athenry on the Galway line, and on to Claremorris on the Westport and Ballina line; this would be of huge benefit to rail travellers in the west of Ireland.

There is now a coach drive of a few miles to Moyasta Junction where the West Clare Railway is now based. Originally the line opened in 1887 and had eight locomotives and 146 other vehicles; it was the last narrow gauge line in Ireland to close when the last train ran in 1961, despite being completely modernised by CIE in the mid-1950s with diesel locomotives and railcars taking over all services. When CIE gave notice in September 1960 of the line's impending closure they said that it was losing £23,000 a year, despite the considerable amount of traffic that was being handled at the time. When it closed on 31st January 1961, CIE started work on dismantling the line the following day.

Moyasta Junction seems to be in the middle of nowhere except for a nearby pub; as far as I can see the nearest place is a village called Doonbeg just north of here. The place is deserted when we arrive and it is a chance

Moyasta Junction, West Clare Railway

for a good look round. The original station building is still intact with a platform on each side and is now used as an office, small museum and booking office. When the building was in operation in West Clare days, part of the building was the stationmaster's house. The station still has its original station name board in English and Gaelic. There is about a mile of track in the direction of Ennis and there are good-quality rails. There is a little signal box some way from the station.

Returning to Moyasta, the tracks pass on either side of the station with the one on the left having two carriages waiting for our trip up the line. In a siding next to them is an old CIE carriage and a Mark 3 British Rail carriage used as storage. The line to the left originally went to Kilrush but beyond the station gate nature has obliterated all signs that it ever existed. There is evidence of much activity with a new concrete platform and reinforcement between the rails in the platform area on the Kilkee departure side. About 200 yards away on this side the line finishes at a fairly busy road; beyond that there is a small mountain of rails ready fixed to sleepers, and it looks as though they intend to push the line on towards Kilkee. The diesel locomotive sitting quietly in the station has a plaque indicating that it was overhauled by Alan Keef Ltd of Ross on Wye, England in April 1999.

There is currently no steam locomotive operating on the West Clare but they have acquired a former West Clare locomotive, No. 5 Slieve Callan, which they rescued from a plinth outside Ennis station and is currently undergoing a boiler overhaul ready for a return to steam.

Due to a mix-up there will be no train ride tonight and it has been rearranged for the morning. In the meantime we are treated to a tour of the inside of the building by Jackie Whelan, who is both charming and knowledgeable. There are many historically interesting things in here including documents and photographs.

There is a very nautical look about Jackie with his white hair, beard and moustache, and he talks at length about his plans for the railway, its history and also its association with Percy French, the famous nineteenth-century songwriter. Percy French was born in County Roscommon in 1854 and in his day was one of Ireland's most well-known songwriters and entertainers; he was also a prolific painter of watercolours.

Jackie recounts the story about the song that Percy French wrote in 1902 entitled 'Are Ye Right There, Michael, are Ye Right?' that derided both the poor timekeeping and the track quality of the railway at that time. The railway company was so embarrassed by the song that it took out a libel action against French, although this failed. The story goes that when Percy French arrived late for the libel hearing in court and was questioned about this by the judge he responded, 'Your Honour, I travelled by the West Clare Railway', which resulted in the case being thrown out. The leaflet produced by the West Clare Railway today proudly proclaims, in italics, the title of Percy French's song about it.

The hotel in Kilkee is quite old but has been extensively modernised and is close to the beach. My room is big enough to accommodate several people, and also has a lovely view of Moore Bay and the wide beach that sweeps round in a graceful semicircle, fronted by villas and cottages. That part of the town has a very Victorian look with its neat villas and promenade.

At the southern end where the headland juts out protectively there is a small harbour with a backdrop of wild hills behind it. The sweeping beach is deserted, and no wonder as despite the fact that it is summer and only late afternoon, the wind is cutting through me like a knife and from the racing grey clouds overhead there is the occasional drop of rain. Despite

Kilkee beach

the weather I can still see why Kilkee built up a reputation as an attractive seaside resort as with warm sunshine and a blue sky this place would be hard to beat.

Back to the hotel, and an extremely nice dinner followed by a pint of Guinness in the hotel bar. Tonight, the bar is being taken over by a wedding party and although everyone is welcome I opt for an early night, but for some reason I cannot get to sleep; maybe it is because I wasn't able to have my bed time coffee. As I lie in bed reading at 1.30 am I can hear that the party is still in full swing.

In the morning I have a chat with the hotel owner. He took this place over a few years ago and came from industry without any hotel management experience, and I have to say that he is making a lovely job of it.

After an excellent breakfast it is time for the short drive back to the West Clare. It is early morning and the little diesel locomotive and its two carriages are ready; the carriages were built four years ago by Jackie and his team and are of the same design as the originals, which had bench seats along each side; it was not until 1948 that this design was changed and carriages were made into compartments. The carriages are showing signs of severe rusting and Jackie says that is because they built them of steel; they are going to replace them for next year with ones made from aluminium.

As we trundle along through the countryside we are treated to anecdotes about the line in its heyday, such as passengers flagging the driver to stop so they could have a pee, and the many occasions when the train would stop at a line-side pub and driver and passengers would alight for a refreshment stop; this was quite common practice, apparently.

The return ride takes about 20 minutes, and along the way there is a field with some cows in it which look quite bemused at our passing; there are also some Connemara ponies frisking about in the next field. A stream with brown trout in it gurgles alongside the line for a short way. The weather and the quality of the track are both good and it has been a very pleasant little ride which will, I am sure, be greatly enhanced when it is done behind the steam locomotive.

Jackie has plans to extend the line to Kilkee, and when I ask him about permission difficulties with the local authority in laying rails across the nearby road, he shrugs his shoulders and says that it will not be a problem as they will just lay them anyway. He is full of stories, and also says that as soon as CIE are finished with something they cut it up so that it cannot be used again. This seems a pity and is part of the reason that the few narrow gauge lines in Ireland have struggled to exist and expand.

There is much handshaking when it is time to go and Jackie urges

Killimer   View from the ferry at Tarbert

us to come again and also to keep up to date via the website, www.westclarerailway.ie. The enthusiasm and commitment to preserved railways by Jackie, Michael and others is something you can only admire.

The next stage is a short drive through Kilrush to Killimer, and from there by ferry across the Shannon to Tarbert, and then to Listowel for a ride on the unique Lartigue Railway, known as the Lartigue Monorail.

Driving through Kilrush there is a very attractive square with trees, neat paving and lots of shops; it is busy with people and looks as though it would be a nice place to stay for a while, but today there isn't time. Kilrush has been designated a heritage town, and with its new marina and dolphin and wildlife centre is now a popular place for visitors. There are also many areas of beauty and interest between the town and Loop Head, where the Shannon meets the Atlantic.

We have passed the towering chimneys of a power station and are nearly at Killimer when a road sign catches my eye; it is a 'proper' sign and says 'Caution – Church Ahead'.

Killimer is really just the place where the ferry arrives and departs but there is a good tourist shop here and a cafe where I can get a cup of tea and a sandwich. I shouldn't really be hungry as it is not long since I had a full cooked breakfast.

The ferry *Shannon Breeze* arrives and drops its ramp on the sloping tarmac for the cars and buses to drive on. The ferry does not anchor but keeps in position by using its engines. The crossing to Tarbert takes about 20 minutes and standing here on the deck high above the vehicle well the wind is very bracing, but there is a lovely view of the Shannon in both directions. There is a very strong current and although the crossing is very smooth the engines have to work harder to keep us on course.

As we drive up the smooth wet tarmac from the ferry we enter the Kingdom Of Kerry. Two or three miles from Tarbert is Ballylongford. This little town is on a creek of Ballylongford Bay on the Shannon, and nearby is Carrigafoyle Castle which was the scene of many battles in Elizabethan times. The Gaelic for Ballylongford translates as 'the ford-mouth of the fortress'. An interesting comparison of well-known people born here is Field Marshall Earl Kitchener, and the father of Jesse James the well-known American outlaw.

We have arrived at the Lartigue Railway in Listowel and are greeted by Tim O'Leary, the stationmaster, who is very welcoming and tells us the history of the railway and shows us several photographic exhibits. The station and its buildings are on the site of the former main line station at Listowel, of which nothing remains except the engine shed which is in pretty good condition; Tim says that they hope to do a lot of conversion work inside the engine shed and turn it into a comprehensive museum about the railway.

Listowel in Co. Kerry used to have an interesting choice of railway in that it had a station on the standard gauge line that ran from Tralee to Limerick and was also the junction for the unique Lartigue Railway which ran to the coast at Ballybunnion some 15 kilometres away. Ballybunnion today is Kerry's premier seaside resort.

The Lartigue railway was the idea of a French engineer, Charles Lartigue, and came about as result of him looking for easier ways of transporting esparto grass across the Algerian desert in the 1880s. After watching camels carrying loads in panniers he came up with the idea of a new type of railway. Instead of the usual double track on the ground he designed and built a railway where a single rail was fastened at waist height on A-shaped trestles with specially made carriages straddling the single rail like the panniers he had seen on the backs of camels. In Lartigue's railway, the 'panniers' were then pulled across the desert by mules.

Although several European railway companies were interested in Lartigue's

Brendan on the Lartigue

Right Away

idea, because it was easier and cheaper to construct that the usual type of railway, nothing came of it and there were only two Lartigue railways ever built. One was in France, but was never used, and the other was at Listowel which when it opened in 1888 had three locomotives and 39 other vehicles. At the time it was the world's first passenger-carrying monorail.

Each locomotive had two boilers and tow cabs balanced on each side of the rail with the driver riding in one cab and the fireman in the other. It is quite incredible to think about what the operational difficulties were in loading freight, cattle and passengers on each side of the trucks and carriages in order to achieve balance. One of the other difficulties was the matter of bridges, since because the railway crossed the country like a fence, special bridges had to be constructed to carry roads over the line. As these were operated by people using the road they were often left open, causing delays and sometimes friction between the railway and the road users. The line was severely damaged in the Irish Civil War and closed in 1924; a small piece of track was saved but everything else was scrapped.

The Lartigue railway of today has been the brainchild of the Lartigue Monorailway Restoration Committee and they have had constructed a new double-sided locomotive and two carriages, together with about a third of a mile of track. Extension of the railway has been hampered by the construction of a new road across the site of the former track. This construction project is remarkable as the original drawings are no longer available, and the gleaming locomotive before me is therefore testament to the skill and ingenuity of the engineers.

With Brendan, the engine driver, on one side and me on the other side for balance we make the short trip to the buffers. Here I have the pleasure of helping him to turn the locomotive on a section of the track that turns

The Lartigue turntable

Brendan the Lartigue driver

He loves his pipe

and slots into place rather like a jigsaw; that procedure is repeated at the other end in order to enter a different platform.

The locomotive is oil fired but that does not take away the fascinating experience of this ride, and with Brendan smiling and puffing away on his pipe while he tells me tales about the railway, the whole experience on the Lartigue has been thoroughly enjoyable.

Listowel is a busy little market town with a one-way street through it. There are some lovely Irish names on the pubs and shops, such as Murphy, O'Donavan, Doyle, Flathin, Mrs Quinn, and the Maid of Erin pub with a huge plaster cast of her above it. The town is also a literary centre and several famous Irish writers have come from this area and a nineteenth-century Georgian house in the town square houses the Kerry Literary and Cultural Centre.

As we leave Listowel for Tralee we cross a bridge over a beautiful river, which I later discover is the River Feale.

I will be staying in Tralee, the capital of Kerry, for three nights and this afternoon there is time to explore this fast-growing town with its population of about 20,000. It is a place famous for its International Rose Festival which is held in August, and contestants for this come from as far afield as America, Australia and the Middle East, as well as Ireland. The famous song 'The Rose of Tralee' was composed by William Mulchinock, who died in Tralee in 1864.

As I stand outside the Ashe Memorial Hall that houses the Kerry County Museum and wonder where to start, I can hear music. It is coming from the town park on my left and turns out to be trio of musicians who are part of a food festival. The clarinet player is really putting his heart into it and then suddenly reverts to vocals, and his rendition of – Bona Sera, Senorita, Bona Sera it is time to say goodnight to old Napoli – Bona Sera *Senorita* kiss me goodnight' is both catchy and very enjoyable. There

Denny Street, Tralee   The Rose Garden, Tralee

are a lot of people about, and the stalls selling different foods are quite busy.

Within this large park is the Garden of the Senses where beds of roses of all colours are in bloom with their different scents drifting past on the gentle breeze: it is indeed a nice place to be.

Out of the garden and across Denny Street is a little park called Pairc an Phiarsaigh, named in honour of Padraig Pearse, poet, barrister, educator and leader of the fight for Irish freedom. It is a quiet little place but it stirs memories of when Ireland was not so quiet.

I make time to look round the museum and it is like a tour through the history of Kerry – particularly through medieval times in Tralee as you can experience the sights, sounds and smells of the community at that time. There is also an exhibition on 'William Melville – Spymaster' who was born in Sneem in 1850. Early in his life he emigrated to England and joined the Metropolitan Police, ultimately becoming the head of Scotland Yard's Special Branch. He was one of the founders of MI5 and was a spymaster known as M and the exhibition details the famous and notorious characters that he was involved with at that time. The 'set pieces' of the exhibitions are very well presented and the models are particularly lifelike. The 'walk-through' experience is both informative and enjoyable.

Walking down Denny Street it is comparatively quiet and I am admiring the lovely Georgian buildings that line each side, but as I reach the Mall at the end it is a different scene with streets crowded with people and the coffee shops doing a roaring trade. Following the road down I come to Rock Street with the prominent Kirby's Brogue Inn which seems an ideal place for lunch, and so it proves as here the humble sandwich is elevated to new heights and the Guinness (or porter as it was called) is superb.

Each pane of glass in the windows that look out on the front are of stained glass and depict different areas of Kerry; one even has a steam locomotive on it. Inside there are some very interesting framed pictures including an Edwardian wedding, a recent Gaelic football match, a railway poster and a poster depicting all the patriots of the 1916 uprising.

As I order my second pint of porter I fall into conversation with the inn owner and he describes Tralee as a good town, with the emphasis on the word 'good'. He has lived here all his life and is very proud of his town and very proud of being Irish.

I am sitting in the middle of Tralee opposite Easons and wondering whether I should have had the second pint of Guinness when two cars drive slowly past side by side while the drivers have a conversation; they seem oblivious of the delay that they are causing.

There will be a lot of travelling over the next couple of days and I will not have much opportunity to explore Tralee further, which is a pity as it is a very interesting town and is well worth a more extended stay.

Tralee is now a terminus for trains from Cork but at one time it not only had a station for the narrow gauge line to Dingle, but it was also possible to continue north through Listowel and Newcastle West to Limerick or south from the Cork line to Valencia. There was also a standard gauge railway line over the eight miles from Tralee to Fenit that was operated by the Great Southern & Western Railway but this closed some years ago. At Fenit Pier there is a sculpture of St Brendan (484–577AD) who was born near Tralee and was the patron saint of Kerry.

It is now two o'clock and time to leave Tralee for the 45-minute drive to Killarney followed by a scenic cruise on Lough Leane; translated from the Gaelic it would be the 'lake of knowledge' or 'lake of learning'.

Killarney is a popular town for tourists and it is very busy today, although the line of jaunting cars near the Methodist church are still patiently waiting for the next tourist. The 27,000-acre National Park surrounding Killarney is probably the most beautiful area in Ireland, and not for nothing is the area sometimes called 'Heaven's Reflex'. With its three lakes, Muckross House, Muckross Abbey and the surrounding mountains including McGillycuddy's Reeks and the Gap of Dunloe, it is indeed a place worth visiting.

A short drive from town is Ross Castle on the very edge of Lough Leane and in front of it is a landing stage from which boat trips around the lake depart. To one side of the lake is a small cafe and they are doing a roaring trade in ice cream. Ross Castle was built in 1340 by the local chieftain O'Donoghue and was the last castle in Ireland to fall to Cromwell in 1652, and standing looking at it today as it towers above me, it is still a very impressive building despite Cromwell's best efforts.

Ross Castle, Killarney

It is during my visit to this part of Ireland that I discover the origin of the green, white and orange of the Irish national flag. It was designed in 1848 by Thomas Meagher and the green represents the older Gaelic and Anglo-Norman elements of the population with the orange representing the Protestant supporters of William of Orange. The white represents peace between the two.

As the boat glides out from behind Ross Island past Inisfallen Island where there was once a monastery that lasted for a thousand years, I can look across towards Muckross Lake or Middle Lake as it is also known, and on its shores is Muckross House which is a Victorian mansion designed by the Scottish architect William Burn and built in 1843 for Henry Arthur Herbert and his wife. It was built in Tudor style with gables and tall chimneys and was visited by Queen Victoria in 1861; it is an extremely attractive building set in beautiful formal gardens full of exotic trees and shrubs.

The view from the boat is really something, with trees and rhododendrons right down to the water's edge and, beyond Inisfallen island, I can see the Purple Mountain (2739 feet) with the towering range of McGillycuddy's Reeks behind; in between these is the Gap of Dunloe, a beautiful glaciated valley with high cliffs and isolated lakes that stretches up from Kate Kearney's cottage to the Black Valley. The Reeks look very stark today against the grey clouds.

The boat is a glass-covered affair but I find it a bit hot in there and opt for the seats at the back where I can sit in the open and enjoy the breeze. There I meet Teresa who is the leader of a flower arranging and cultivation group from Cork. There are about ten of them and they are very noisy and there is much laughter. Teresa asks me about places in North Wales, and is it as nice as Ireland? She can really talk and it is not difficult to see why she is the leader of this group, although the rest of them are by no means shrinking violets. One of them accuses her of having kissed the Blarney Stone and when I casually ask if she was born in Blarney the whole group dissolve into laughter. Like all the Irish people that I have met so far they are both friendly and welcoming.

Back at the hotel I enjoy the luxury of its four-star accommodation followed by a superb meal. The hotel is on the edge of a retail and trading estate and the area is quite quiet and a little way out of Tralee and I decide to give the town a miss and catch up with my notes and do a bit of reading, not forgetting to water my arbutus bush that I bought five days ago and is destined for home. What the person who cleans my room thinks of the 3-foot bush in the bathroom I am not sure.

It is six o'clock on a sunny Sunday morning, the sky is blue and the grass is shimmering with the early morning dew. Across the cloudless sky I can see the vapour trail of a single aeroplane. The plan for today is to trace the route of the former Tralee & Dingle narrow gauge railway along the north side of the Dingle Peninsula as far as Castlegregory Junction, where a branch went to Castlegregory, and then through the hills via Glenmore and Annascaul to Dingle on the southern coast.

The Tralee & Dingle Light Railway opened in 1891 with eight locomotives and 108 other vehicles. It eventually closed in 1953 and today all that remains of this very interesting line is a 2-mile section from Tralee to the famous windmill at Blennerville; this windmill was built in 1800 and is still working today. During the famine of 1845–48, Blennerville was the main port of emigration from County Kerry, and the visitor centre on the windmill site has an interesting display on Irish emigration at that time.

The Tralee to Blennerville Railway (made famous in the Michael Palin TV series *Great Railway Journeys of the World*) is unfortunately not running at the present time because of problems with the locomotive. When the Tralee and Dingle railway closed, its locomotives were moved elsewhere and one of them, Hunslet 2–6–2 number 5T, was sent to the Cavan railway and when that closed 5T was shipped across the Atlantic to the Steam town museum at Vermont. Years later it was rescued and brought back to Kerry and restored, and in 1993 began life again on the relayed track of the Tralee and Blennerville Railway. Number 5T is the only surviving locomotive from the Tralee & Dingle Light Railway.

The journey out of Tralee by road or rail is very picturesque with a canal on one side of the road and a river to the sea on the other side, and up ahead the mountains of the Dingle Peninsula. On Tralee estuary there is a lovely bird sanctuary where birds from Northern Europe come to overwinter. In addition to the many wading birds here it is also possible to see herons, cormorants and guillemots in addition to the many swans that have a home here.

We are now near the point where the branch line to Castlegregory left the Dingle line and the road has narrowed and is descending into a valley with a very narrow bridge that crosses the River Finglas (Finglas from the Gaelic meaning 'clear stream') at the bottom, the road then curves away up the hill.

As we cross the river, on the left is a reminder of the old railway: Curraduff Bridge. Covered in ivy, it stands testament to the engineers that built this line long ago and it now looks like some ancient monument, which I suppose it is. It was also the scene of the worst accident in the history of the Tralee & Dingle when, in 1893, a special, carrying pigs and a coachload of passengers, ran away down the bank towards the bridge and the locomotive leapt the curve on the approach to the viaduct and plunged 30 feet into the river below, taking most of the wagons with it. Luckily the coach lodged on the parapet of the bridge and did not fall, but three men and several dozen pigs were killed.

There is short roadside stop to take in the view and it is really something, for from this high point we can look down on the beautiful plain spread out below that stretches to the waters of Tralee Bay and beyond. In-between there is a pattern of beautiful fields criss-crossed with hedges and scattered with little houses and farms. The sky and the sea are very blue, the fields are very green, the sun is shining and the view is enchanting. It is a lovely moment.

The road now turns away from the coast and heads inland across the peninsula and more or less follows the track of the railway. Both the old track bed and the road are now lined with fuchsia bushes, the flowers of which were described to me by one Irishman as 'Christ's tears'. The clouds are chasing across the blue sky and making ever-changing patterns on the green fields where the sheep are grazing. The view is very peaceful and rather timeless.

We have arrived at Anascaul. For a small town it seems to have a lot of pubs, including Dan Dooley's shocking pink pub, The South Pole Inn in blue and white and The Randy Leprechaun which is painted in fluorescent lime green. There is also a house painted in the most vivid red and yellow you can imagine; they certainly like bright colours here, and why not?

The road is now twisting and turning as it climbs higher before dropping down into Dingle. I like the warning signs painted on the road on the approach to a narrow S-bend: the first says 'Slow', the next one 'Slower' and the one after that 'Very Slow'. We are just passing a lovely little cottage with the garden a blaze of colourful flowers and along the top of the garden wall is a long line of ornamental deer.

We have arrived in Dingle (An Daingean) and I have about three hours to look round. The construction of the marina here has been completed but this seems to be the only change since my last visit some 15 years ago, apart from the new Tourist Information Centre where I am now looking for cards and presents. The selection here is excellent and I settle for a tee shirt for my granddaughter with the message on the front reading: 'Someone who loves me bought this in Ireland'. From talking to local people I have discovered that the Tourist Information Centre occupies the site where the railway turntable once stood.

Dingle is renowned for traditional music and fine seafood and is the capital of Kerry Gaeltacht (the Irish speaking area) and while I am here I manage to learn three phrases in Gaelic: 'Conas ta tu' (how are you), 'Le do thoil' (please) and 'Mile buiochas' (thanks).

The whole area around Dingle is steeped in history and perhaps one of the most well-known sights is Gallarus Oratory, an 800-year-old early Christian church that is still in perfect condition; it is close to the village of Murreagh, north of Dingle. There are very many ancient monuments and archaeological sites in and around Dingle, and just east of Slea Head is the 2,000-year-old fort of Dun Beg. Where Slea Head pushes out into the Atlantic, it is the most westerly point of Ireland.

Strand Street along the sea front of Dingle is lined with pubs and restaurants and as it is near enough lunchtime I pop into Gavin O'Grady's Marina Inn and enjoy an excellent plate of fish and chips, together with the usual superb pint of Guinness.

An advertisement in a nearby fish and chip restaurant says: 'Assistant wanted, fluent English a necessity'.

Beyond the front in a quiet nearby street is a small bookshop. It is painted a vivid blue and plaster models all over the front give the impression of dolphins jumping out of the building itself.

Wandering into a craft and bookshop called Leac a'Re (moonstone) I get into conversation with Tony and Eileen. In answer to my question about the posters that I have seen around the town, they say that it is a campaign to persuade the local authority to promote and prioritise the use of the original Gaelic name for Dingle, which they wrote down for me as Daingean Ui Chuis.

The Dolphins

Daingean Ui Chuis

They are very interested in my railway travels and as I stand reading one of their books about railways they apologise for not having any about the Tralee & Dingle railway but Tony says that he can get one from Danno for me to look at. Danno turns out to be the owner of a restaurant and bar in Strand Street (speciality, sweet chilli prawn tails) and apparently has a large selection of railway books. When Tony returns he says that Danno is out but he has managed to get in the house and find me a copy of the *Tralee and Dingle Railway*. I am quietly reading this when Danno appears; he is a tall man and speaks with a lovely soft Irish brogue and is here because Tony has asked him to come and see me about his books. He leaves some more railway books with me and says to return them when I have finished. The friendliness and trust of these people is wonderful and is a good memory to take away.

Three hours isn't really enough to explore this town and I haven't had time to visit Upper Main Street, the Town Park or the Craft Village but I am sure that I will return to Daingean Ui Chuis in the not too distant future.

Dingle shop window

Dingle harbour

Church in Dingle

On the way to the minibus and opposite a petrol station on the edge of town there is a plaque set into a wall that reads:

The Tralee and Dingle Light Railway. It ran thirty-one miles from Tralee to Dingle Pier, the most westerly railway in Europe. Construction began in 1888 and opened in 1891, its purpose was to stimulate the economic life of the area and it was a unique road side railway, a great deal of it was unfenced and abounded in steep curves and gradients of 1 in 29 to 31 as well as 70 or more level crossings, mostly ungated. A branch line, also 3-foot gauge ran 6 miles to Castlegregory, passenger services to Dingle ceased on 17th April 1939, goods trains and monthly cattle specials continued until it finally closed in 1953.

This plaque was placed here by the Dingle Historical Society in 2006.

The plaque in Dingle

The return journey to Tralee will be straight across the peninsula via the Conor Pass. The road out of Dingle very soon becomes steeper and narrower, and looking back after only a few minutes I can see Dingle and the bay spread out behind me like a picture postcard with some tiny white sails on the water and little white dots grazing in the patchwork of green fields far below.

As we get higher the mountains are very green but it is still bleak and there are very few trees. At the top of the pass there is a viewing point and an enterprising soul is here with an ice cream van. The view from here is something special as behind me I can see far away to Dingle Bay, while in front of me, and far below, the land stretches to Brandon Bay and Tralee Bay which are spilt by a small peninsula with beautiful sandy beaches on each side. Almost at my feet and far below are the still blue waters of Lough Gill.

The road down from the pass seems steeper and narrower than coming

Tralee Bay

up from Dingle but the driver has got his foot down as though he is late for some vital appointment. It is an uncomfortable but exhilarating ride.

We have reached The Railway Tavern at Camp and mine host is Michael O'Neill: he is one of the Men o' the West and appears on several postcards. With his hair cascading down to his shoulders, rampant beard and moustache and two very piercing eyes he is a formidable-looking person, but as I talk with him this image is dispelled as he is friendly, welcoming, knowledgeable and a pleasure to talk to.

Mike – The Railway Tavern, Camp

He is a mine of information about the Tralee & Dingle railway and indeed, also puts a DVD about the railway on the television for the interest and enjoyment of locals and visitors alike. When I tell him of my difficulty in obtaining a book about the railway he disappears and returns with an out-of-date but new and very comprehensive book which he presents to me; in return I promise to send him a copy of my book about my railway travels in South America. Mike's pub is very traditional and full of atmosphere and interesting items and souvenirs of all kinds, including items relating to railways. It was a pleasure to meet him and share a Guinness and count him as a new friend.

Outside the pub and looking across the road, it is hard to imagine that there was once a railway station and junction here, for as well as the long-gone station buildings there was also, in addition to the through line, a passing loop and several sidings. There are now just two reminders of the railway here, one is a plaque on an old piece of the platform which commemorates the crash of 1893 and the other is the original water tower. Legend has it that while T&D train crews were watering their locomotives at this point they also spent time watering themselves at the hostelry opposite.

Mike and Keith talking railways   The Railway Tavern at Camp

Monday morning dawns grey and overcast and the forecast for southern Ireland is for a lot of rain. Today is the train to Cork and Cobh via Killarney and Mallow, and then a drive back to Tralee.

Tralee station is a grey block-like building with a glass conservatory-type building on the front with seats for people to relax in. Inside it is a two-track terminus with a signal box at the end; it is a very functional station without being attractive.

When the railway used to terminate at Fenit the trains continued through where the buffer stops are now and then across the Listowel road for the eight miles to Fenit Pier, The extension to Fenit eventually closed in the 1970s.

The train is very busy and I am wedged in on all sides by members of the Irish Country Women's Association who are travelling to Termonfecking, north of Drogheda. My nearest companions are Doreen who is from Waterville on the ring of Kerry, and Abby and Helen who are from Killarney. They have travelled with many others and there are also some from Tralee itself. The train seems absolutely packed with women discussing their forthcoming day out, and they are as excited as bunch of children who have been promised a treat. They will be joining others from all parts of Ireland and are meeting for a two-day seminar which will include needlework, flower arranging, cooking and many other skills. Thanks to my passion for cooking I am able to hold my own in conversation with them and the time passes quickly and pleasantly. Most of these ladies are travelling free, as bus and rail travel in the Republic is free once you reach the age of 66: a passport is free once you reach 70. The last piece of information that they give me before we part at Mallow is that the dolphins have arrived in Dairbhre (Valentia Island), and that that is a good sign for local prosperity.

The line from Tralee has been following the road but as we leave

Farranfore station the line veers away into what is a very wild-looking piece of country until we approach Killarney station where there is a very interesting manoeuvre. The line approaches the station on a bank high above and I can look down on the passengers waiting on the platform below: the train carries on for about half a mile and then reverses into the station, picks up the passengers and then continues to Mallow. Because the line from Mallow to Tralee was built by two separate companies, which met at Killarney, it became a terminus; trains to Tralee have to reverse out of the station before heading westwards.

The run from here to Mallow is very fast and smooth and it seems no time at all before we arrive at what is in effect a railway crossroads; it is a very busy junction with several platforms and from here trains go to Tralee, Limerick, Dublin and Cork.

The two-car unit that I am on and that I thought I would have to change from at Mallow is actually now going straight through to Cork. There is a tunnel as we approach Cork and I time our journey through it at two and a half minutes, but unfortunately did not find out how long it was. There is a sign over the tunnel that says: 'The light at the end of the tunnel – Murphys'.

Cork is a very interesting city and easy to explore with its heart being an island between two arms of the River Lee. In this heart, picturesque bridges and quays, from the days when the river played a major part in Cork's prosperity still remain and add to the charm of the city. Near to the Red Abbey, the oldest building in Cork, on George's Quay is Fitzpatrick's secondhand shop where it is said that if they haven't got it then it probably didn't exist. There is much to see and do in Cork but unfortunately no more time today as visits to Cobh, Macroom and Killorglin have to be fitted in before returning to Tralee.

Cork station is a very busy, efficient, bright and clean place with gleaming terrazzo floors and a glass roof in the booking hall. There is a train waiting to depart for Dublin and it a very smart-looking affair with gleaming paintwork and equally gleaming power cars at each end; our train to Cobh will however be more modest as it is a two-car unit from the bay platform.

In a corner of the hall is a preserved locomotive standing on a section of original Great Southern & Western Railway flanged rail. She is No. 36 and was purchased from Berry, Curtis & Kennedy in Liverpool for £1,955. The wheels are on a 2–2–2 arrangement with a 6-foot driving wheel; she weighed 19 tons and was based at Inchicore works running shed and her working life from new was pulling passenger trains at up to 60 miles per hour from 1847 until she was finally withdrawn in 1874; her final mileage was 487,918.

No. 36 appeared at the famous Cork International Exhibition of 1902 and the railway centenary exhibition of 1925 and she was finally placed here in Cork Kent station in 1950. Her very last outing was in 1958 as part of a unique exhibition of railway locomotives and rolling stock at Inchicore works in 1958, and today she stands here with her gleaming green paint and shining copper dome as a testament to the railway pioneers of the past.

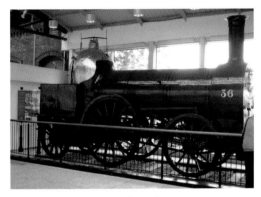

Number 36

The train is on time, of course, and as we pull out of the station the rain is lashing down, and after running alongside the wide estuary for some time we arrive at Cobh some 25 minutes later when the sun comes out as though to greet us.

Cobh is situated on Great Island, one of three islands in Cork harbour, and is linked by rail and road causeways. After Queen Victoria visited here in 1849 the town was renamed Queenstown but reverted to its original name in 1921.

Cobh waterfront

The square at Cobh

Poster of the old Queenstown station
at Cobh Heritage Centre

SS *Servia*, Cobh

Trains from Cork now use the top end of the original platform while the Victorian main entrance, booking hall, waiting rooms and offices have undergone a lovely restoration which now also includes a restaurant, gift shop and an informative and enjoyable audio and visual presentation: it is now called the Cobh Heritage Centre.

There is a lovely photograph on the wall inside taken at the turn of the last century, showing the interior of the station. Looking at it now I can see that if you removed the chairs and tables of the present-day restaurant from the old booking hall area it would be an identical view. There is also a plaque on the wall as you go in that reads:

> After the rising of 1798 over six hundred united Irishmen were transported to penal colonies in Australia where they subsequently influenced the department of the democratic and egalitarian ethos of the Australian nation.

The audio/visual presentation is very interesting and there is a wealth of information about the history of Cobh including emigration and the sea tragedies associated with town.

The mass emigration from Ireland was because of poverty, crop failures and the lack of opportunity and it reached its height following the total failure of the potato crop in 1846. Between 1848 and 1850 about 2.5 million Irish men, women and children emigrated from Cobh.

Just outside the Heritage Centre there is a bronze statue of Annie Moore and her two small brothers; the statue is close to the water's edge and one of the brothers is looking seaward towards the New World while Annie gazes back at the country that she is leaving. Annie and her brothers sailed from Cobh on 20th December 1891 in the SS *Nevada* and when they arrived at Ellis Island in America they were the first emigrants to be registered there. The statue is a symbol of the many Irish who made that same difficult and perilous journey. I am standing next to that statue and finding it very difficult to imagine the huge number of people that passed this way.

Emigration of another kind also took place at Cobh when in 1791 the first convict ship, the *Queen*, sailed from Cork harbour with 159 prisoners on board bound for Australia. In the next 60 years nearly 40,000 men and women were sent to Australia as convicts.

Cobh, or Queenstown as it was known then, is perhaps most well known for being the last port of call for the ill-fated *Titanic* before she went to the bottom of the Atlantic after hitting an iceberg in 1912. One hundred and twenty-three passengers embarked at Queenstown, and as they waited in the tenders PS *Ireland* and PS *America* at the Deepwater Quay while mailbags were loaded, the *Titanic* rode at the outer anchorage just off Roches Point. The Deepwater Quay is next to the old railway station, or Cobh Heritage centre as it is now known, and I am now standing on that spot trying to visualise that scene from long ago.

By the entrance to the audio/visual presentation there is a model of the Cunard liner SS *Servia*, and while I cannot see what scale it is, it is about 8 or 10 feet long. She was built in Glasgow in 1881 and was the first liner to be built of steel. She weighed 7,392 tons, was lit by electricity and carried 1,000 passengers. The SS *Servia* was the largest vessel ever to berth alongside the Deepwater Quay at Queenstown and was eventually scrapped in Preston in 1902.

A little way up the coast from here and just off the Old Head of Kinsale the Cunard liner *Lusitania* was sunk by a German torpedo in 1915. She was carrying 1,959 passengers and crew and despite a lot of rescue boats, only 761 people were saved.

The town centre of Cobh is just up the road from here and on my way I pass a very pleasant little park on the waterfront. There is a bandstand with a pagoda-style roof and on the grassed area between some pretty flower beds are some ancient cannons, possibly left over from the time of the Napoleonic Wars.

Looking across the now sun-dappled water of the harbour I can see Haulbowline Island with its Martello tower, and Spike Island which was once used as a prison.

There is a lovely square with Georgian houses on both sides and small shops; St Colman's cathedral looks down on the square and the winged angel monument that I can also see is in memory of those people who lost their lives on the *Lusitania*. Beyond the cathedral and high above the town is the Old Church Cemetery where some of the victims of the *Lusitania* sinking are buried in a mass grave, many of them never identified.

Walking back I can see across the road what was once an elegant house. It has the words '1910 AD Soldiers Home' etched in the stonework, but below that is now a Chinese takeaway.

The town of Cobh is a very attractive little place with its small shops and elegant Georgian houses and it nestles peacefully up against the waterfront. As I look back from the Heritage Centre it is difficult to equate this lovely spot with all the anguish and heartache that passed through it all those years ago.

The drive back towards Cork is very pleasant as we follow the tidal estuary and we have just crossed a lovely old bridge. Across the estuary I can see a train slowly crossing its own bridge over the water on its way back to Cork.

Half an hour from here brings us to Macroom which is an attractive and thriving market town, but as I stand outside the town hall with its clock tower and weather vane it seems as though all the traffic in Ireland is passing through in an almost constant stream of trucks, coaches and cars. Across the square is what I would describe as an old-fashioned hardware shop which seems to have everything you could need for your house and garden. Inside the town hall there is a lovely old meeting room with rich wood-panelled walls and a plaque showing the names of past and present town councillors.

The town hall is just a little way from a street called Railway View but the trains of the Cork & Macroom Direct Railway, which opened in 1866 with four locomotives and 132 other vehicles and covered the 24 miles from Cork to Macroom, have long gone.

Macroom Town Hall

There must be something here that I need

Despite the traffic, the town of Macroom has a beautiful setting in the Lee Valley with the River Sullane flowing through it to the rear of the castle ruins; all that remains of the castle is the Norman tower and some parts of the wall. The original castle had a long and chequered history and was thought to have been built in about 1220. By the 1500s it was owned by the McCarthys of Muskerry and over the following 200 years was besieged many times; both Cromwell and Charles II had a hand in deciding the ownership of the castle. It eventually became the property of Olive White in 1800, who subsequently became Lady Ardilaun after she married Baron Ardilaun in 1869; he was perhaps better known as Arthur Guinness.

Ownership of the castle eventually came to the people of Macroom through a trust but in 1967, after years of neglect, the building was in such a condition that the local council had it demolished. The entrance with its archway and twin towers survives, and outside there are some ancient cannons facing the square.

The Castle gates at Macroom

I get into conversation with a man on the square selling fruit and vegetables and he seems as knowledgeable about the history of Macroom as he is about the price of apples.

I think that Macroom is a place where you could spend a lot of time as there is much of interest to see and do, including a visit to nearby Bealnablath where Michael Collins was shot in 1922, The Gearagh close to town where there is a wildlife sanctuary and the remains of an alluvial forest and, on the other side, the famine graveyard at Carrigastyra.

It is nice to sit back and enjoy the drive through the lovely countryside as we head for Tralee, passing through places like Clonkeen and Glenfesk and eventually Killarney, but we are not stopping here this time and have moved on to Killorglin.

The sun is shining as we approach Killorglin and I think what a pretty little town it is; nestling on a hillside with the River Laune at the bottom it looks a very inviting place.

The river runs alongside the main road and just before we reach the lovely old arched stone bridge that crosses the river into the main square there is a bronze statue of a Puck Goat on a plinth. The main square is the central point for the Killorglin three-day Puck Fair in August which is probably the world's oldest and is certainly world famous. On the first day of the fair, known as the Gathering Day, a wild male mountain goat is paraded through the colourfully decorated town and then taken to a three-tier stand in the square where he is placed on the lowest tier of the platform. This is followed by the Puck Fair Queen delivering the Puck Proclamation which bestows the freedom of the town under the patronage of King Puck to all those present. The Queen then places a crown on the head of the Puck Goat, following which he is raised to the full height of the platform, which is about 50 feet, from where he can look down on his fun-loving subjects for the next three days.

The second day is for the livestock sale of horses, cattle and sheep and this usually commences at about 4 am. On the third day, known as the Scattering Day, the goat is taken from his pedestal and paraded through the town once more; he is then released back into the wild. I attended this fair back in 1991 and it was a truly memorable event.

Killorglin used to have a train service which first travelled from Farranfore and crossed the viaduct over the River Laune in Killorglin, known locally as the Metal Bridge, on 15th January 1885. The line then went through to Valentia but was eventually closed in 1960.

It has been a long day and I can feel my eyelids drooping, but we are soon back in Tralee and after a shower and a change into a clean shirt, I feel rejuvenated and ready for another excellent dinner.

The morning has dawned grey, wet and miserable and it is an eight o'clock start; at least it is not cold. The plan for today is to drive to Limerick and catch a train from there to the famous Limerick Junction, change, and then take a further train along the scenic route through Clonmel to Waterford.

The countryside is very lush and green and we have just passed through Castleisland where Crag Cave is situated. This beautiful cave was discovered by cave divers in 1983 and there is a wonderful display of stalagmites and stalactites.

The run north takes us to Newcastle West which is an attractive market town, and alongside the road into the town the River Deel flows over a weir and some rocks and then disappears under a beautiful old bridge.

We have nearly reached Limerick and have now made a short stop at Adare, which is rated the prettiest town in Ireland. In the Heritage Centre there are some lovely pictures and photographs of old Adare and it is interesting to compare them with today's refurbished buildings and thatched cottages, which I think give the town a slightly manufactured and touristy air, but it still looks nice. The colourfully painted shop fronts on the wide main street are however very typical of Irish towns and look extremely attractive.

Just outside the town, and we are passing a luxurious hotel and golf course complex where the Irish Open was held recently. The hotel is a huge Victorian Gothic mansion and was built in 1832 by the 2nd Earl of Dunraven on the site of a previous mansion.

Leaving the village, the road crosses the River Maigue via a bridge built in the nineteenth century. With its many arches and recessed areas to protect pedestrians from traffic it retains the charm, if not the construction, of the original wooden bridge that was built in about 1400.

Like most of Ireland there is a lot of history in Adare, and just beyond the bridge are the ruins of Desmond Castle built sometime before 1226. It rests snugly against the banks of the river.

Limerick, Ireland's third-largest city, is a world away from Adare. We are not stopping here and are heading for the station. On the way I can see a council worker brushing rubbish at the side of the street; he is making a good job of it despite the fact that he is keeping one hand in his pocket while he does it – he is a picture of casualness.

Several of the streets that we are passing through have some extremely attractive four-storey Georgian houses; there are also a lot of reminders of Irish patriots, such as the Wolfe Tone Bar.

Close to Shannon Airport and straddling the river Shannon, Limerick was built on the foundations of a Viking settlement; the Vikings arrived in 831 and developed Limerick into a trading port and despite many battles with local chieftains they managed to hold the city until in 967. They were eventually defeated and driven out by Mahon, brother of Brian Boru who was the founder of the Dalcassians, a powerful tribe in that area which predated the Vikings.

Perhaps the greatest events in Limerick's history were the two great sieges by the forces of William III in 1690 and 1691, when the defence of the city was organised by General Patrick Sarsfield. His name has long been revered as the gallant defender of Limerick. When the war ended in 1691, the Treaty of Limerick was signed, which was followed by 'The Flight of the Wild Geese', the name given to Sarsfield and his 10,000 Irish Jacobite soldiers who marched out of the city and embarked for France.

Limerick is still a busy place and in railway terms has lines to Ennis, Dublin via Nenagh and Waterford via Tipperary. There is also a freight-only line to Foynes on the Shannon estuary. Between 1939 and 1945 Foynes was the main point for flying boat traffic between Europe and America and the Flying Boat museum there details this era. The first part of the line to Foynes uses the track bed of the former Limerick to Tralee line.

The line to Ennis originally continued north to Sligo with links to Galway at Athenry, and Westport at Claremorris along the way; that route is now known as the Western Railway Corridor and I understand that there is a possibility that the Athenry and Claremorris links will be restored in the not too distant future. This decision would no doubt be helped by CIE's policy of leaving track in situ and/or retaining ownership after passenger and freight services have been withdrawn.

This is perhaps a good time to mention that the combination of Partition and the closure of all narrow gauge lines in the Republic resulted in there being no train services north of Sligo or in County Donegal. There is talk about extending the line north from Sligo through Ballyshannon, to Donegal Town, Letterkenny and then east to meet up with a new line from Derry towards Letterkenny. This would restore Donegal's rail link with the rest of Ireland and would be particularly welcome at this time of population and tourism expansion.

There is a pleasant park next to the station, which is yet another grey stone affair but with a nice clock in the middle; the foyer inside is a very clean and modern affair with gleaming floor tiles and a glass-fronted information office, where train information is clearly displayed. There is a very nice restaurant as well as a refreshment kiosk. The place is busy.

Brand new at Limerick

I go for a stroll to the end of the platform to take a photograph and there on a siding are two brand new inter-city units awaiting service: the seats still have their plastic wrappers on.

There is a woman staring with some fascination at the information boards while round her are three young children making various demands that include ice cream and chocolate; without her apparently being aware they are steering her in the direction of the refreshment kiosk; it is a bit like watching tugs trying to berth a liner in a dock. I must be staring, as she turns to me and asks about the next train to Thurles. As luck will have it I can tell her as it will be the same as I am catching. I tell her about my rail journey around Ireland and she chats about her sister. Her accent is very soft and pleasing to the ear and she wishes me well for the rest of my trip and she is surprised and pleased when I say that I hope her sister's troubles are sorted out OK.

For me the interchange with strangers in another land is an integral part of the journey and lends quality and interest to the experience. This has been particularly so for me in Ireland, a country that I have a lot of affection for.

Everywhere that I have been to in Ireland so far shows evidence of the substantial investment that has been made in terms of track, stations and rolling stock and on the way out we pass a big engine shed with yet more new units stored in it; there is hope for the Western Railway Corridor yet.

Another excellent initiative in Ireland is that the bus and train services are integrated and link with each other for times and places; the bus stations are nearly always part of the railway station.

It is just a 20-minute ride to Limerick Junction and as usual the scenery between towns is very green and rural; there are some horses gambolling in a field, kicking their legs up and shaking their heads. In a seat opposite me is a man with an extremely long beard and a large walking stick that is completely covered in red elastic bands; maybe he collects them.

We have just arrived in a wet and windswept Limerick Junction. In that short journey we have passed several castles and I later discover that there are over 700 castles in County Limerick alone. Limerick Junction is a very long, open place and is an island platform with a couple of bay platforms, one of which contains our train to Waterford. It is also a place where trains are marshalled and there is a huge long tanker train hauled by two locomotives. Considering that it appears to be in the middle of nowhere, Limerick Junction is a very busy place in terms of trains with three sitting here at the moment and two having left already, and that is just in the ten minutes that I have been here.

Inter-city at Limerick Junction

Freight at Limerick Junction

This is the point at which Dublin to Cork trains cross the Limerick to Waterford line at right angles, and our single-car train now reverses out of the station back towards Limerick and then forward across the diamond crossing on its 90-minute journey to Waterford, with Tipperary the first station, about two or three miles away. The Limerick to Waterford line was completed in 1854 and is one of the oldest routes in Ireland; it is the only non-Dublin intercity route and after a period of many years is now due to have a realistic service.

Tipperary station is by a road junction and is a shadow of its former self with a derelict goods shed and a very small platform and station building. Nobody gets on or off here. We have just exchanged the single line tablet and are on our way; it is still very wet and masses of dark clouds are chasing across the leaden sky.

We are now heading towards Cahir and most of the journey is through deep tree-lined cuttings with the occasional glimpse of farmland and beyond that, the mist and cloud-shrouded Galty mountains; in some places you can see the forestry covered slopes steaming as the temperature rises. There must be a lot of crossings as the locomotive horn blares out frequently.

There is a big new bridge over the river just before Cahir station and presumably this replaced the original viaduct which had a bit of a chequered career with two incidents involving long periods of closure of the line. The first in 1955 was when an out-of-control train crashed through the buffers of the station loop and through the deck of the viaduct; the driver and fireman were killed in that incident. The second incident occurred in 2003 when a train of cement hoppers became derailed and part of the train was dragged through the deck cross-sections; the locomotive and driver managed to cross safely.

Just before the bridge there was a good view of the lovely Cahir castle – Cahir from the Gaelic which means 'stone fort'. The fort originally stood on a island in the River Suir close to the town. Conor O'Brien, Lord of Thomond, built a castle on the site of the fort in the twelfth century which was subsequently incorporated into the Anglo-Norman fortress that succeeded it. It was renovated and extended in the fifteenth century and sixteenth century and remained in the same family until 1964.

Looking down from our high vantage point above the town the view is very attractive with nice houses and neatly laid out gardens; it looks a very nice place to visit.

The station however is not much to look at with its derelict goods and engine shed long closed and two old loading bays with their lines long gone. Nobody gets on or off at the small station except the guard who appears to be acting as postman as he delivers a letter to a nearby house. At the line side there are huge stacks of brand new modern sleepers as if to confirm Irish Rail's commitment to this line.

After Cahir the view of the countryside is arable and more open and we are just passing an impossibly green field with one or two brilliantly white cottages dotted about. If you painted a picture of this vivid emerald and white scene I am sure that it would be considered unrealistic.

It is only a short distance to Clonmel and the area in between is rich with broad-leafed trees. There is a small industrial estate and lots of houses on the edge of town and it is obviously quite a big place, as befits Tipperary's main town. The station was obviously larger at one time but now looks small and a little stark, although quite a few people get on here. There is a nice homely feel to this part of the journey as the driver has sounded his horn to several people along the way who he obviously knows.

I have a copy of George Borrow's book *Wild Wales* at home and it is interesting to learn that he spent some of the happiest days of his boyhood in Clonmel, fishing for trout in the river and rambling over the hills. Clonmel was also the place where he gained his first knowledge of the Irish language in the Grammar School that then was just outside the West Gate. The West Gate was rebuilt in 1831 and today spans O'Connell Street. The town itself is very ancient and was formerly walled. When Cromwell came here in 1650 contemporary accounts said that he never experienced a more severe repulse that he did here, and he lost over 2,000 men. Another famous writer associated with Clonmel was Laurence Sterne, author of *Tristram Shandy*, who was born here in 1713.

Leaving the station I can see a large stack of old rails on sleepers and a man busy with an acetylene torch cutting them up. It is more evidence of the upgrading of this line but it seems a pity, as I am sure that some of the narrow gauge lines that I have seen so far would be only too glad of them.

From there to Carrick-on-Suir it has been mostly arable land but with the brooding and mist-shrouded Comeragh Mountains in the background. Carrick is a small market town nestling on the banks of the River Suir with the station some way out of town to the north, and you get the impression that nothing much happens here. But there is Ormond Castle, the finest surviving Tudor manor house in Ireland.

Alongside the station is a railway preservation society which preserves old locomotives. They only have diesels and from a brief glimpse from the train you get the impression both that there is very little money and that nothing much happens there.

The railway has been following the river for some time but by a small town called Fiddown (which used to have a station but it closed a long time ago) it suddenly heads due south while we continue east to Waterford. Just beyond Fiddown the countryside is very remote and passing a lonely farm I can see in the corner of a field another piece of history – it is a Mark 1 Cortina.

We are now on the edge of Waterford and the contrasting view is a bit brutal as there are bulldozers and diggers everywhere, cutting out huge swathes of grassland for what looks like a large road interchange for the new bypass that is also under construction.

Slowing down to enter the station we pass the signal box, and as we do the driver hurls the single line tablet to the ground; there is no question of passing it to the signalman. The town is on one side of the River Suir and the station is on the other side. The station is compact, clean and modern and is wedged between a cliff face and the river. The station entrance faces onto an incredibly busy road junction and as I step out I

Waterford station   Outside Waterford station

also face driving rain and an easterly gale; it is obvious that my small umbrella is no match for the elements.

Crossing the very open bridge that leads to the town the wind seems to increase in intensity and whips the top of the brownish grey river into a milky froth. I end up walking crab-like in order to try and keep my back to the wind. It is extremely wet and Waterford is aptly named today.

It is Ireland's oldest city, being founded by the Vikings in 914. When the Anglo-Normans eventually wrested the city from the Norsemen they rebuilt and strengthened the city walls and also rebuilt Reginald's Tower, the walls of which are 10-feet thick. I pass this tower on the way out of town, situated at the junction of The Mall and the quay; there is an inscription on it that says it was built by Reginald the Norseman in 1003. Driving slowly up The Mall there are some lovely Georgian houses to be seen. Today there are plenty of examples of the original walls to be found in those parts of the city that were included in the area fortified by the Vikings, including the Watchtower at the top end of Parnell Street.

Away from the town, near the yard of the former Tramore railway station there is a tower with embrasures and crenellated battlements which is in a very good state of preservation.

Tramore is a seaside place with a beach about two miles long and is south of Waterford. It was originally served by rail when the Waterford & Tramore Railway opened in 1853 with four locomotives and 32 other vehicles, but the service ceased many years ago; it was narrow gauge and just over seven miles long.

Waterford has a long history of trade and is still one of Ireland's busiest ports. Although we are quite along way from the actual harbour I can see tied up, not far from the bridge, a light ship, a few trawlers, an old lifeboat and miscellaneous other craft.

The main part of the town is about half a mile from here and as I head

The Bandstand

up Bridge Street and then Barker Street I come to what is almost a village green with some shops around it and a bandstand in the middle. It is too wet to linger and moving on past nearby Patrick Street there are some good remains of the original city walls.

Off the High Street there is a new and modern shopping precinct and despite temptation because of the rain I manage to resist going round it; time is again short and as I didn't come to Ireland to see a shopping centre that is probably like any other, I head for the quay as I have noticed one or two interesting hotels along there and I am ready for some lunch.

On the way there is a very interesting-looking bookshop and the display of old books, magazines and posters is partially obscured by small grimy windows: the place has a very Dickensian look and I find it irresistible. The owner is not only friendly and happy to talk but is also interested in railway history. He tells me how a few months ago he came across the original drawings and layout for Tramore station and the line from Waterford; he goes on to say quite casually that he put them in the window for sale and they went quite quickly. He seemed surprised at that but was very coy about what price he had asked for them. Considering that the line was opened in 1853 those documents are of great interest to both historians and railway buffs alike.

He, like most of the other people that I have met so far, is proud of his town and likes to talk about it and tells me things to look out for; he does concede that it rains a lot. Unfortunately, there is not much selection in terms of books about Irish railways but he has been very interesting to talk to so I feel obliged to buy something and settle for a 15-year-old *Visitors Guide to the Paignton & Dartmouth Railway*.

There is a very inviting-looking hotel on the quay and I get into conversation with the chef while I order a beef sandwich; apparently they are not doing sandwiches – only meals but with the typical friendliness and helpfulness of the Irish, he says that that is no problem and proceeds to carve an extremely generous helping of beef from an enormous joint. He then asks the girl who is waiting on to take it into the kitchen and make it into a sandwich. When it comes, there is so much beef, bread, salad and chips that it no longer seems appropriate to call it a sandwich. I do manage to finish it, but it is a close thing.

The chef has never been to Wales and we talk about the nice places that he could visit. He wants to go to Cardiff to watch the Irish play Wales at rugby and says that it is not so much the game that he enjoys but the social interaction with fellow Celts. I think that translates into a hard drinking session.

It is time to go and I am glad of the opportunity to sit back and let that enormous lunch go down on the short drive from here to Kilmeadan for a ride on the Waterford & Suir Valley Railway.

On the way out of town we pass the famous Waterford Crystal factory. The business was started by William and George Penrose in 1783 but in 1851 it was forced to close because of draconian taxes. A new factory was opened in 1947.

The Waterford & Suir Valley Railway is the longest and most scenic preserved railway in Ireland, and it runs for about four miles from Kilmeadan station to Carriganore along part of the former Waterford to Cork line through Dungarvan. The original line opened in 1878 and closed in 1967, but following the construction of a new factory at Dungarvan the line was reopened in 1970; unfortunately when that factory closed in 1982, so did the line.

The present narrow gauge railway came into being in 1998 with a partnership of organisations and eventually opened in 2003. The aim at the moment is to reinstate the line to Waterford about five miles away but

Kilmeadan station

59

that has been delayed by the construction of the bypass; nevertheless there are hopes to reach Waterford by April 2009.

The amount of rain today has been phenomenal and the road is flooded in some places but despite the weather I am impressed with my first sight of the Waterford & Suir Valley Railway set-up: it is neat, tidy and well set out, and gives the impression of being professionally run and maintained. It is a single line with a loop in the station, and our train is at the platform. It consists of a restored Simplex locomotive that originally came from the north of England and two open-sided carriages which today have plastic curtains to keep out the rain.

First things first and a nice hot cup of coffee in the refreshment and souvenir room, which is actually an old inter-city coach.

Not long after leaving the station the line closely follows the River Suir for the rest of the journey, and despite the rain it is possible to appreciate the fine view on the other side of the river with the rolling farmland and the mountains behind. At the river's edge are the remains of Kilmeadan Castle which in 1649 was taken and destroyed by Cromwell, and the owner hanged from a nearby tree. The line passes through the Mount Congreve Estate, with its many greenhouses and beautiful flowers including hundreds of rhododendrons and camellias, and then past the site of the recently discovered remains of a Viking settlement. Although I got a couple of nice photographs of the station, I don't get any along the line as every time I lift the plastic flap I get a face full water either from the rain or the water that is pouring off the roof. Despite the rain, this has been an enjoyable journey and it would be nice to do it again, although preferably when the sun is shining.

Back at Waterford station for the 45-minute journey to Kilkenny, and it is still raining. There is only one stop on the way, at Thomastown where one of Ireland's most luxurious hotels is situated. There is also a nice railway viaduct over the River Nore dating from 1877. It is 212 feet high and replaced the original timber one that was constructed between 1846 and 1850.

The arrival at Kilkenny is not very encouraging as the sky is grey and overcast; it has been raining and is now just starting again. Sheltering under the faded blue paintwork of the front porch of the hotel the prospect seems a little bleak and gives no indication of the wealth of history and interest in this town.

I don't usually go beyond a brief comment about the hotels that I stay in but, in my opinion, this one is a bit special. The Club House Hotel is a lovely building over 200 years old with wonderful Georgian architecture, detailed plasterwork, thick carpets, beautiful polished wood floors and elegant brass fittings, and it has an atmosphere of eighteenth-century elegance throughout. There are many corridors, and on the walls there is a fascinating collection of 'Spy' cartoons. Sitting in the dining room with its high ceiling and ornate plasterwork it is not hard to imagine yourself in another age.

The Club House in Kilkenny

There is a plaque in the hall and the following is some of the information from it:

The Club House was an Inn from the 1790s and owes its name to the fact that for almost a century it was the headquarters of the Kilkenny Hunt Club whose exploits in the pursuit of foxes were rivalled only by the boisterousness of their diners in the hotel. The manager of the hotel in the 1860s recalled one evening during which John Courtenay of Ballyellis, County Cork, rode his horse up the stairs and jumped over a screen in the dining room for a bet of £50. The Kilkenny Hunt Club which was founded in 1797 by Sir John Power of Kilfane, used the original Georgian building as a club house until it was converted into the Iberian Hotel and Fox Hunting Club in 1817 to coincide with the construction of the new Cork road. The hunt still gathered in front of the hotel for its annual opening meet up to the 1960s when it had to be abandoned because of traffic disruption.

After a few Guinnesses last night and a full Irish breakfast this morning I think it is essential that I spend the rest of the morning exploring this town, not just for its considerable historical interest but also to work off some of the considerable number of calories that I must have taken on board.

In the thirteenth century Kilkenny was the medieval capital of Ireland and today it is one of Ireland's loveliest cities. Kilkenny Castle by the River Nore was built in the 1190s by the Normans. There are still some alleyways surviving from medieval times, and these are known locally as 'slips', such as the Butter Slip where butter stalls used to ply their trade; nearby there is the Market Slip as well. It is also a brewery city and today there are still over 70 pubs including Kyteler's in the very narrow and quaint St Kieran Street, which was once known as the most famous old inn of Kilkenny.

There are plenty of lovely old buildings in Kilkenny and I will try and see as many as I can before my train leaves for Newbridge at 11.27 am. First of these is Rothe House in Parliament Street which is a fine Tudor building that was originally the home of a wealthy Irish merchant and dates from 1594; it consists of three town houses and is now a museum, bookshop and library, and I spend some time inside as there are some wonderful historical documents and artefacts. I end up with a nice poster of famous Irishmen.

Wandering back down the High Street I spend a few minutes browsing in a bookshop and in a corner there is a stool with a notice on it saying: 'I am a stool, please sit on me'.

Across the road is the Butter Slip; it is a steep lane with many steps and connects the High Street with St Kieran Street below. Nearby is The Tholsel (Town Hall), a large and interesting building that was built in 1761 and used as market place at that time; it has a very Italian look about it.

I take the short cut down the Butter Slip and at the end on my right is the Shee Alms House in Rose Inn Street that was founded in 1582 by Sir Richard Shee and was to accommodate 12 poor persons. Today it

Rothe House

The stool in the bookshop

A 'slip'

houses the Tourist Information Office, but this is not yet open which is a pity as it would have been nice to see the inside. The small windows look out on a narrow and very busy road that leads to the town centre; one of the staff has just arrived and is trying to shelter from the rain in the lee of the building while attracting the attention of her colleagues inside – she is not having much luck.

Just after passing the Shee Alms House, and I am crossing St John's bridge over the River Nore and on a man-made floating island in the middle of the river, under the shadow of Kilkenny Castle, is a magnificent display of flowers; it is a blaze of colour and very attractive.

I want a bit of time at the station so keep on going up John Street until I reach the junction with Wolfe Tone Street and Dublin Road; across the road is the station and an enormous building site. On the way I have passed some pubs with a lovely collection of names including Matt the Millers, Biddy Earlys, Breathnach's and O'Faolain's.

The station is undergoing many changes, with a new booking office and waiting room and although the top end of the platform is still there the

Shee Alms House

Kilkenny Castle from St John's Bridge

63

Kilkenny pub window

rest of the old buildings have gone as part of a large development that will include apartments and retail outlets. The old station buildings were on a high level above the road and although the original station buildings have gone the original high brick frontage is still there and it looks as though they are going to incorporate it into the new development, which will be nice.

Although Kilkenny is on a through line from Waterford to Dublin it is effectively a terminus, as the line that used to continue through the station and on to Portlaoise has been gone for some time and trains to both Waterford and Dublin via Carlow now reverse out of the station for their onward journey to both destinations, a bit like Killarney. The Gaelic sign on the station footbridge reads: 'Na trasnaiteer ach thar droichead coisithe' or 'Cross the railway by footbridge only'.

Suddenly there is a lot of activity as two trains arrive, one for Waterford and one for Dublin; one has been held on the single line while the other runs around its train using the loop in the station. It is all very quick and

Old Kilkenny station

One for Dublin and one for Waterford

easy and we are soon on our way: it is a locomotive-hauled train and very comfortable, as usual.

I think that, along with Tralee, Kilkenny is one of the most interesting and attractive towns in Ireland with its interesting little shops, cafes and elegant and historic old buildings.

As we reach Muine Bheag station I am again reminded of the impression that you get in Ireland, when you travel by train, of enormous areas of beautiful green fields and woods and trees and very few houses. This trip makes you realise that Ireland is much bigger than you think it is when you look at a map. The original station platform here has a modern extension indicating the increased loadings on this line.

Carlow is a very attractive mustard-coloured station with lots of chimneys; there are also lots of people waiting on the platform. A crowd of women have joined the train here and the tranquillity of the carriage that I am sitting in is suddenly shattered as what seems like a hundred noisy females take root in it. There are actually eight or nine of them, it just seems like a hundred. They are from a bowling club in Dublin and have been on a short break at the Talbot hotel in Carlow and they are now sharing their experiences of their time there. They are loud and their language is quite choice and I am wondering whether it is a prudent move for a lone male to engage them in conversation, but nothing ventured, nothing gained. They don't find the idea of somebody travelling round Ireland by train very fascinating and have now started to tell me about their experiences in the evenings. One of them, I forgot all the names as they came at me in a bit of a rush, says that her short break had contained all that she had wished for which was a hot bubble bath, a glass of wine and a man. Her wish had been granted when room service had delivered a bottle of wine to her room one night when she was in the bath.

They mostly live in north Dublin and when I tell them that I have a friend in Artane, it turns out that one of them knows him, although not very well; it reminds me of the old cliché about a small world. We talk about Dublin and an old haunt of mine in Abbey Street, the Oval. Why am I not surprised when most of them say that they know it? They ask about places in Wales, as it seems that none of them have ever been there, and the time passes very quickly, so much so that I seem to have missed Athy and Kildare stations and we are pulling into Newbridge station where I get off.

Newbridge is an attractive and original station, but there is no time to linger as there is a coach ready to make the journey to the the Steam Museum at Straffan about five miles away. There is just time for me to use the toilet on the station and through the tiny booking office window I ask for the key, which is an old-fashioned affair which opens an equally old-fashioned door and lets me into a toilet straight out of the last century, but it is extremely clean and well kept.

The journey does not take too long and as we approach the entrance through a country lane there is a sign that says it is 400 paces to the museum. The museum is housed in a very attractive old church with a pointed bell tower; this church was originally a Great Western & Southern

Straffan Steam Museum

The gardens at Straffan

Straffan Steam Museum

Railway church at Inchicore and was moved here brick by brick and opened as a museum by President Mary Robinson in July 1992.

There is a fascinating collection of model locomotives and actual size and original steam pumps, boilers and engines including a boiler designed by Richard Trevithick (1771–1833) for his high-pressure steam engines. Richard Trevithick's first two models are no longer in existence but his third model is here in Straffan.

All the model locomotives are in the Richard Guinness Model Hall and were made before mechanical drawings were in general use. All around the hall are portraits of the early inventors and engineers such as Isambard Kingdom Brunel (1806–59), James Watt (1736–1819), William Dargan (1799–1867), Ronald St Charles Parsons (1864–1931) and, of course, the two Stephensons, George (1781–1848) and Robert (1803–59).

The locomotives are housed in attractive glass and polished wood cases and there are about 20 of them including the following:

London, Tilbury & Southend Railway, 4–4–2, $4^3/8$-inch gauge.
Great Western Railway, *City of Bath*, no. 440, $2^1/2$-inch gauge.
Great Northern Railway, no. 120, 4–2–2, $3^3/4$-inch gauge.
Liverpool & Manchester Railway, 2–2–0, $4^3/4$-inch gauge.
Shrewsbury and Chester Railway, long boiler no. 240, $4^5/8$-inch gauge.
Great Western Railway, no. 1114, 2–2–2, $4^3/4$-inch gauge.
Great Western Railway, broad gauge, no. 422, $5^1/8$-inch gauge.
Caledonian Railway, no. 2, 4–4–0, $3^5/8$-inch gauge.
North Eastern Railway, no. 901, $4^1/4$-inch gauge.

In an adjoining hall are all sorts of steam-driven items including a Duplex Steam Pump from Jameson Distillery, a steam-generating set from a naval corvette circa 1929, a single-cylinder horizontal engine which was new in 1900 and worked until 1976 and a triple expansion marine engine from the SS *Divis* built in Belfast in 1928. It is a really interesting place, particularly as some of the engines are in steam and working for our enjoyment and interest. The whole interior of the building with its lovely high timbered ceilings is beautifully kept and presented and it is possible to spend a long time here.

The museum is adjacent to the Lodge Park Walled Garden which is marked on the map as a place of particular interest; it was built in 1777 to provide the Palladian House with flowers, fruit and vegetables. The sun is now out and it is lovely to stroll round this garden with its different themed areas such as the White Garden with its central wellhead. There is also a yellow and blue border, and I am at the moment looking at a plant that I cannot identify but is a bit like a large flax with a tall stem from the centre on top of which is an almost black flower; it is both attractive and a bit forbidding.

There is only one more night's stay in Ireland before I have to return home, but before that there is a visit to the Irish National Stud at Kildare.

Travelling on the N7 from Newbridge to Kildare we are passing the Curragh, a grassy plain in County Kildare that covers about 5,000 acres. It is all unfenced and part of it is also home to the world-famous Curragh racecourse where the Irish Derby takes place. Not far away, I can see three horses being put through their paces with the jockeys bent low over the necks of their mounts.

Around the gravelled car park of the National Stud are some extremely elegant trees including a beautiful greyish-blue Atlantic pine and several gold and purple Japanese acers. The reception area is very busy, and after purchasing tickets, a young man from the staff scoops up a group of us for a tour of the site. Just outside the reception building there is a beautiful lake with willows drooping down to the water, and on a grassy bank at the edge of the water there are some small cygnets huddled together fast asleep with their heads tucked under their feathers while two swans sit close by in watchful mode. The whole area is immaculate with velvet lawns and lots of trees and colourful flowers. There are also some gunnera plants that I haven't seen since I was in Cornwall years ago, and in the background there are towering chestnut trees. The lake is fed by the river Tully and mallard and kingfisher reside here and there are some golden wagtails in the bamboo grove at the water's edge.

Our young guide is a mine of information and is relating some of the history of this place. It was founded in 1900 by Colonel William Hall-Walker who was the son of a Scottish brewer, and the guide tells us that many things have been said about the Colonel's horse-breeding methods, which have included 'preposterous' and 'inspired': this was mainly because he sold his foals on the basis of their astrological charts. Hall-Walker gave the stud as gift to the British Crown in 1915 which, in turn, gave it to the Irish Government in 1943. Later the Irish National Stud Company was formed, which still runs the stud today.

The whole site covers about 1,000 acres and our first stop is at a paddock where there are two graceful-looking horses gently cropping the grass. Our guide introduces them as Vintage Crop, winner of the Melbourne Cup, and Florida Pearl, winner of four Gold Cups. They don't race any more and are kept in this paddock as a tourist attraction.

Vintage Crop

Nursery paddock

Is this my best side?

Swan and chicks – National Stud

The foals are born between 14th and 15th July, and the following year they are all given a first of January birthday and become yearlings. All the horses here are thoroughbreds.

There is a foaling unit where mother and foal are together for a time until the foal is transferred to another paddock where there is a mixture of younger and older foals; I am standing by this paddock and it is lovely to watch these spindly-legged creatures frolicking about.

In a solitary box we meet the stallion Tommy the Teaser: it is his role to test whether the mares are in season rather than let them go to the stallion first. This is to prevent injury to valuable stallions but it must be a frustrating job for Tommy.

As we walk along, the young man continues to pour forth information including how to identify what colour is classified as chestnut and the colours that identify a 'bay'. There is a lovely oak tree-lined avenue with paddocks on each side but they are empty today, and then just round the corner we have reached the stallion boxes.

Tommy the Teaser

The lake – National Stud

The Irish National Stud

It is interesting to learn of the relationship between the racing success of the offspring and the stud fee; this is illustrated by three boxes in front of me where each stallion has his offspring information on a brass plaque on the door. The stud fee for each of these glossy looking animals is different, being 3,500 euros, 10,000 euros, and 15,000 euros for the one at the end, who is Verglas. The top stallion on the site is Invincible Spirit whose stud fee is 35,000 euros; his offspring had 35 separate race winners between them in 2006.

The walk round the stud was both interesting and enjoyable but it is also nice to relax now on the veranda of the cafe here and enjoy the sight of ducks on the lake, especially when they turn themselves upside down to look for food under water and just leave their legs sticking up in the air.

Back to the hotel now and a nice dinner, followed by probably my last Guinness on this journey, and then the train to Dublin Heuston station in the morning.

The last day dawns a bit grey and it is drizzling; we are sitting in Kildare station at the moment and there is a delay caused by an incident at Heuston station. The trains are quickly stacking up for Kildare which is the point at which trains from Cork, Waterford, Tralee, Galway and Westport all converge onto the same line into Dublin; it must be a bit of a logistic nightmare for the train controllers. There is another train at the platform here and passengers in each train stare at each rather like goldfish in a bowl. The delay has been about half an hour, but when we eventually pull into Dublin Heuston we are only a few minutes late.

Outside the majestic frontage of the station it is teeming with people – tourists, shoppers and travellers – and it is here that I see for the first time the LUAS light rail system. They are modern electric trams and there are two separate lines connecting the southern suburbs of Tallaght and Sandyford with the city centre.

The line to Sandyford uses some of the track bed from the old Dublin and South Eastern Railway Harcourt Street station to Bray line that closed in 1958. Although it duplicated the coastal line to Bray it did serve an ever increasing suburban population and even in 1958 there was much disagreement on whether it should close. It is good to see that that mistake has now been recognised and that places like Ranelagh and Dundrum now have a rail service again, although housing development beyond Sandyford may preclude the line extending further and linking up with the coastal DART line.

I am using the Tallaght to Connolly station line, and so it seems is everyone else. We all cram on; well, not all as quite a few are left behind: I think that even the Japanese train attendants could not have squeezed any more on board, but they do run every eight minutes anyway so there is not long to wait for another.

This trip is exceptional value as for about £1 it takes me across and along the side of the River Liffey that runs through the heart of Dublin, down Abbey Street (remember the Oval) and across O'Connell Street in the heart of the city and arrives at Connolly station about ten minutes later; it is a very stress-free trip across a congested city.

I climb up the steps to the refurbished, bright, clean and modern station of Dublin Connolly and looking down I can see the gleaming electric tram below that brought me here from Heuston station. It is interesting to compare it with the ancient nineteenth-century narrow gauge steam locomotives that are being lovingly restored elsewhere in the Republic; it seems to make the rail system of Ireland one large working museum from the 1860s to the present day. To me it also sums up the great strides

The LUAS at Connolly Station

forward that Irish Rail has made with its transport system. In addition, its programme of line reopening is also evidence that Irish Rail recognises some of the short-sightedness of past line closure decisions and now sees real benefits in infrastructure enlargement.

This journey for me has been one of discovery and enjoyment. On this trip I have travelled all of the rail lines to the west and south of this country and nearly all of the others; during that time I have seen lovely towns and cities and have come face to face with both history and beautiful countryside. I have met fascinating and lovely people, all of whom were willing to talk and listen to this man from another land and answer his questions, and as I sit here in the departure lounge waiting for the boat to Holyhead I can't help feeling sad to be leaving. But I am sure that the pull of Eire will ensure that I return in the not too distant future.

2

Scotland 2003

Sunday, and it is not a very good day to start out on a journey around Scotland by train. There is a problem with trains in my area and rather than risk waiting for the replacement bus, which didn't stop at my station last time, I opt for a lift to Chester, planning to catch the bus from there to Crewe.

The bus finally arrives. It appears to be already full and the vague outline of faces peer out through steamed up windows. It seems that there are about five seats for the 25 passengers waiting to get on and there is much muttering amongst our little band on the pavement.

Suddenly, the majority of the passengers already on the bus decide that they want to get off for a smoke and a walk round, this is despite the fact that the bus is already running late. The driver says that nobody from our group can get on until the smokers have returned to their seats; this announcement is not greeted with any enthusiasm.

Finally they start to return and our group decides to board the bus as well.

The bus now has 80 people on board (it seats 53) and the driver orders off everybody who is standing. The bus is full of swearing and cursing people who are falling over luggage that is everywhere (the boot is already full). It seems a miracle that I have not only got a seat but the front one as well! The driver resorts to subterfuge, saying that there is another bus in ten minutes. Most of us don't believe him.

We are under way and the two young Irish men on my right are part of a family of four which includes a mother and small girl sitting behind myself and my companion. The little girl soon gets bored and decides to play a tattoo with her hands on the back of our seats. The lady next to me whirls round and screams at her to stop; in doing this she bangs her arm on my case, which I have on my knee, and immediately tells me to

73

be more careful. The two young men tell her to shut up and leave the little girl alone, mother joins in and there is a united threat, from the family, to throw her off the bus. The driver appears to be perspiring more that the temperature warrants. The young men lean over and tell me 'that woman has been like that all the way from Holyhead'; maybe they wanted me to sit there as a sort of buffer zone.

The Irish family are travelling from Galway to London and we soon have an interesting conversation going about Ireland and why they are leaving – work apparently. The lady next to me changes tack and becomes know-all and argumentative about everything that is being said. The temperature rises again.

We arrive at Crewe after what seems like an eternity and I bid farewell to my temporary travelling companions. I am catching the 13.20 to Glasgow Central and when it arrives there is plenty of room and I choose a table seat with an elderly couple at the table seat across from me. His accent is broad Glasgow and hers, broad Cockney. They have two half-gallon containers, the contents of which are undoubtedly influencing the man's conversation! They start a fierce argument about whether Preston is the station where you change for Blackpool.

A young girl enters the carriage; she is wearing a very long double string of pearls and a tee shirt with the motif, 'I can only please one person a day'. Underneath it says, 'Today isn't your day'.

The elderly man nods off for a while and when he wakes up the couple start an argument about bagpipes: she says that she can't stand them and he tells her to shut up. He asks me for my opinion and I say that I like them; he promptly joins me and then proceeds to tell me his life story.

He tells me that he was in the South African Police for 20 years and the Army for 20 years with the Inniskillen Fusiliers in Cyprus and Northern Ireland. He says that he is currently working as a printer. It is not clear whether this is true as his wife shouts across 'You are not working now', and he makes a coarse reply.

I fall into conversation with a journalist opposite me. She works for the BBC, specifically writing short stories and poetry. I mention that I write short stories and we become engrossed in conversation and the time passes quickly until suddenly we are in Glasgow, ten minutes late. It is more than 25 years since I last saw Glasgow Central station but the only things that seem different are that it is busier and cleaner than I remembered. The nice old wood panelling is still there as is the old Central Station Hotel, although I am sure that it has been refurbished since I was last here. I have nice memories of the Central Hotel but have no time to look inside as I have to catch the 18.10 from Queen Street station to Stirling.

It is only a short walk to Queen Street station but I get there only to find that the 18.10 has just left. I hope that this is not an omen for the rest of my journey. I speak with one of the station staff who tells me that the next train for Stirling is at 19.40. He is very pleasant and helpful and regrets that I have missed the 18.10. This was to be the start of the very favourable impression that I got of Scotrail throughout my tour of Scotland.

The station is covered by a big iron and glass roof. The terrazzo floor is extremely clean and there is no litter anywhere, even though there are no litter bins! The whole place is immaculate and there are plenty of shops offering food, drink and information.

Glasgow Queen Street station

I am never bored sitting on railway stations and the wait is not unpleasant. When the train does arrive, I reflect on how clean and smart it is, with tinted glass, comfortable seats and free reading material.

I can see nothing outside as it is quite dark and I relax and read until we arrive at Stirling just after 8 pm.

The directions to my lodgings had seemed straightforward and I walk up the hill from the station into town; the weather forecast is right, it is starting to rain. All the shops are closed but plenty of them are lit up and there are no security shutters so I can window shop as I go. The walk takes me through the main part of the town centre, some of which is pedestrianised. Melville Terrace is situated just beyond the town centre on a raised level above the main road.

It is a lovely old Georgian house (built 1805) with a few steps up to a typical Georgian front door; there is a very elegant interior with a curved staircase up to the first floor. My room has a double bed which is a bit on the small side but very comfortable and big enough for just me. The furniture is solid and old fashioned, but good quality.

I sleep like a log and come down refreshed to a superb cooked breakfast. Outside the window is a beautiful long back garden with a pond and a permanent resident heron. A couple are staying as well, he is English and she is German. They talk at their two small children in both languages at once: it must be very confusing for them. He appears to be all hair with just two eyes and a nose peeping out. Snow is forecast for the North, I used to think that this far up was the North!

Stirling has always been one of the most important towns in Scotland and in medieval times the castle guarded the main crossing point over the River Forth. It was said that 'To hold Stirling was to hold Scotland' and because of this, the town became known as 'The Key to the Kingdom'. Stirling Castle is open to the public all year round.

Outside of the town is the Victorian Gothic monument (220 feet high) to William Wallace, the greatest of Scottish patriots who spearheaded the movement which finally established Scottish independence in 1314. Although William Wallace was defeated by the English at Falkirk in 1298, and later executed in London, his famous victory over the English at Stirling Bridge in September 1297 was the spark that lit the flame for Robert the Bruce to eventually lead the Scots to freedom when he defeated Edward ll's army at Bannockburn in 1314.

For £1 I can leave my case at the bus station while I have a walk around town, even though it is continuing to rain. You could shop and spend a lot of money in Stirling as it is a very interesting and compact town and has something for everyone. There is a recently refurbished Victorian shopping arcade with shops that complement its style and also a modern shopping arcade with designer shops and other well-known names. In

addition, there are plenty of places to eat or just have coffee. The Old Town Jail, Lady's Rock, Stirling Harbour and the Old Kirkyard are all worth a visit.

It is time to retrieve my case and head for the station to catch the 12.09 to Aberdeen, where I stop for the night. The station building here is clean and litter-free and is a well-preserved example from the nineteenth century with glass and iron roof covering. The WHSmith newsagent on the platform has its original curved timber frontage; I have not seen one like this for 30 years.

Stirling station

The railway runs on the east side of Stirling and before long we are north of Dunblane where it is wild moorland with nothing else to see except the odd cottage in the middle of nowhere.

We have reached Gleneagles where the view outside is of great tracts of heather stretching as far as the distant mist-shrouded hills. The whole scene has an almost primeval air about it; there is certainly no population explosion in this part of Britain.

The train is quite empty and quiet except for the rushing sound as it speeds through the rain. Dunblane and Gleneagles are the only stations still open between Stirling and Perth and there is a long tunnel into Perth followed by grey tenements backing onto the line, then suddenly a very impressive river and frontage.

Perth station is very large and dark with a lot of platforms and is a railway crossroads serving Glasgow, Edinburgh, Dundee, Aberdeen, and Inverness. It still has the old-fashioned signal boxes and semaphores but there is an impression of efficiency.

We have left Perth and are now running alongside the Perth–Dundee road and appear to be racing the cars, and winning! It's pouring down with rain. There can't be a better way to get from Glasgow to Stirling to Dundee to Aberdeen. There is a nice view of the airport alongside the railway just before we enter Dundee, no jumbos here though. The station is quite modern and is built on a lower level to the street above.

Dundee is now the permanent home of RRS *Discovery*, the ship that took Captain Scott to Antarctica. *Discovery* was launched in Dundee in March 1901 and after two expeditions to Antarctica and voyages to Russia, Spain, France, USA, Holland, Turkey and Canada, she finally reached her permanent home in 1986.

RRS *Discovery*

The Old Steeple in Dundee is also worth a visit as it is the tallest surviving medieval church tower in Scotland. The city itself is a thriving, bustling place with all the shops you could want including the brand new Overgate Centre. You can even meet Desperate Dan in Dundee, as he is immortalised by a large bronze statue in the main shopping area.

There is a long tunnel out of the station and then we pass the docks with what looks like large factory fishing ships. It is still throwing it down with rain.

The Old Steeple

We pass the little seaside town of Broughty Ferry with a shingle beach and caravans, mostly of the old-fashioned type. The town has a fine esplanade and sweeping sands but today the sea on our right-hand side is very grey and choppy and covers those sweeping sands.

The harbour is the venue for the traditional Ne'er Day Dook; this is the annual Tay crossing swim held on 1st January in which bathers attempt to cross the icy waters to Tayport. I'm sure that it can't be any colder than it is today!

Lovely coffee and smoked ham salad served from the refreshment trolley, but it does mean that my attention is diverted from Monifieth station. The settlement here dates back to the ninth century and it is thought that it was once an important Pictish centre.

There is the briefest of stops at Carnoustie which hosted its first Open Golf Championship in 1931.

It is open country on one side with damp fields and grey and white cattle and the grey and angry sea on the other side until suddenly, just before Arbroath, there is Focus DIY and McDonald's; a bit of a stark contrast.

Arbroath is a more extensive station than I thought it would have been and had obviously been an important railway point at one time. The town is associated with the Declaration of Arbroath of 1320 asserting Scotland's independence from England and also has substantial ruins of a monastery founded in 1178. Today it is the largest town in Angus and is both a holiday resort and a fishing port. A famous delicacy of the area is the 'Arbroath Smokie', but today I will not be able to sample that delight.

The line north of Arbroath is now on cliffs high above the sea and it is a spectacular view. Montrose station, when we arrive, is very wild and windswept. Montrose is a Royal Burgh and the town is situated at the mouth of a tidal lagoon which is a wildlife sanctuary of international importance. There is a huge supermarket by the station and a lot of little ducks playing by a swollen brown river. North of Montrose I can see cart horses grazing in a field, a lovely sight.

The quality of the railway track is really excellent and the train is travelling really fast. It is chucking it down with rain and even at this speed I can hear it beating on the windows.

Stonehaven looks very grey and gloomy in this terrible weather but it is a nice spot by the sea with its enclosed bay and pretty harbour and seafront. I can just see a sweep of sand through the rain but the coastline is mostly very craggy here.

Nearly into Aberdeen, and we have just gone under the airport flight path with a big jet flying quite low. The first sight of Aberdeen is high-rise flats and an industrial estate; the view could be the 'backside' of any big city in Britain until suddenly there is an impressive bridge over the river approach to the station, a bit like Perth.

The concourse at Aberdeen station is a great domed hall with a glass roof supported by many iron girders and like all the stations that I have seen since arriving in Scotland, it is spotlessly clean, with a gleaming tiled

Aberdeen station

floor. The severe weather warning and advice not to travel unless absolutely necessary that has been issued by Scotrail appears to have done the trick, as within ten minutes of my train arriving the concourse is deserted.

Outside, the station is not quite so glamorous, as the entire frontage is a car park. The lovely old iron canopy that goes all the way along the front of the station is a shadow of its former self, as all the glass has long gone. This is particularly tragic today as it is still pouring down with rain, and the cash machine that I need is not only under its glass less roof but, almost by design it seems, is directly under a leaking gutter. I am forced to try and manipulate the machine with one hand while holding an umbrella with the other.

In trying to find the tourist office I follow the signs, only to discover that they seem to be sending me back the way that I have come. Eventually I find it, although purely by accident. It has an obviously new carpet and I derive some satisfaction by standing on it, dripping water. I ask for a street map and they charge me 50p! I always thought that Scottish meanness was just a myth, until I discover that it is the same map that was in the free brochure that they had sent to me at home. I later discover an Aberdeen joke: 'An Aberdonian went to London to spend a holiday – and that's all he spent'.

My first impression of Aberdeen, apart from it being very grey and very wet, is that it is big, busy and overpowering. Everything seems to centre around Union Street which runs through the heart of the city from Holburn Junction to the Castlegate. There is traffic everywhere, and people as well, despite the rain.

I head for Union Terrace Gardens which on the postcards is very attractive but today is damp and forlorn; there is however a nice church spire framed between green, gold and red trees. It is only an illusion, as when I walk on I find that it is just that, a spire. The rest of the church has gone as though crudely ripped away by some giant's hand; in its place there is just waste ground and a road.

Church, front and back

Behind me is His Majesty's Theatre with its great green dome topped with the flag of Scotland. In front is a truly magnificent statue of William Wallace standing proudly on his granite plinth.

I make my way past Robert Gordon's college and the Art Gallery, but with the rain still pouring down I decide to take cover in the Bon Accord Shopping Centre for a bit. It is very new and very modern but there doesn't seem to be anywhere to get a cup of coffee. As I am talking to a man in a mobile phone shop, my phone rings. It is nice to have the comforting link with home, especially when I am told that it is a beautiful day there!

Aberdeen was founded as a Royal Burgh in 1124 and it has a long association with the sea. The streamlined clippers of yesteryear that served the China tea trade have long gone and it is now about oil. Oil executives from all over the world now live and work in Aberdeen. It is a quintessentially northern city and it is said that the granite makes buildings sparkle after the rain. I can't confirm this as it has not stopped raining since I arrived!

To the south of the city is Duthie Park and the Winter Gardens; here is the all-round warmth of a floral display under two acres of glass, said to be the largest covered display in Europe. It is a pity that my time schedule will not allow me to spend time there, as although my topcoat is keeping out the rain it would be nice to walk round a dry and warm garden!

I am walking down Broad Street on my way to Provost Skene's House; this is an elegant sixteenth-century town house with an aura of style and elegance. Regretfully, how to get in defeats me, and when I mention this later in the tourist office I get the laconic reply, 'Aye, it is a bit difficult to find the way in.' She goes on to explain certain doors and passageways which lead to the entrance, but the moment has passed.

With Aberdeen's maritime history I decide that the Maritime Museum will be worth visiting and on the way I pass Marischall College in Upper Kirkgate (the largest white granite building in the world). To me it is a long, tall grey building with many windows and spires and, although undoubtedly impressive, I find it somewhat forbidding.

Marischall College

The Maritime Museum is shut! For the season, for the week, for the day, who knows? Time to head for my lodgings to dry off and get a hot drink; it will be a miracle if I do not catch a cold. Aberdeen and Grampian is known as Whisky Country. Perhaps I should have toured the distilleries rather than the town!

I find my lodgings down a gloomy and deserted side street and although my room is quite big, it is very basic after Stirling. I am right opposite the Samaritans, which are housed in a very grey and forbidding building, and I wonder if the welcome matches the surroundings!

I didn't sleep well last night. The bedroom wall is paper thin and I heard every sound from the next room, even whispers! It didn't help having a bright street light right outside my window. I have to make a drink crouching on the floor as there is no table. The next horror is that the toilet has not been properly cleaned since the last occupant, and I decide that I will stick to hotels in future.

A good, hot Scottish breakfast goes some way to restoring my spirits, but outside the wind is gale force and it is still raining. I resolve to leave Aberdeen two hours earlier than planned and hope for better weather farther north; the forecast says no chance!

I call in at the railway information centre to ask about the travel situation; the staff there are very pleasant and helpful. I resolve that I must write to Scotrail and praise the standard of service and cleanliness that I have encountered.

There have been no trains south of Edinburgh for two days because of flooding; funny how Edinburgh seems a somewhat remote place from here. Like London seen from North Wales.

I am catching the 11.40 instead of the 13.12 and the guard announces on the speaker system that there will be a few minutes' delay while they wait for the train from Glasgow which has been held up because of floods. He follows this up by walking down the train and apologising, and assuring us that they will do their utmost to make up the time. I thought that this sort of service on the railway had passed into history!

The line from Aberdeen to Inverness gets flooded periodically at Elgin but is OK at the moment. I later find out that the section between Elgin and Keith was closed because of floods a few hours after I had passed through.

The first stop out of Aberdeen is Dyce. There does not seem to be anything remarkable about Dyce other than that it is the station for Aberdeen airport. It is very busy and a lot of people leave and join the train; the majority of them appear to be connected with the oil industry.

The River Don follows the railway as far as Inverurie and it is in full flood and very brown with peat. As a railway town, Inverurie is a shadow of its former self but still has a very attractive station building dating from the beginning of the twentieth century. The Great North of Scotland Railway Company had, at one time, a very large works here and many steam locomotives came here for repair and overhaul, including *Sir Nigel Gresley*.

Just north of Inverurie I catch a glimpse of a castle in the mist. The surroundings are now very remote but suddenly we are at Insch. This seems to be a small village in the middle of nowhere, but no less attractive for that. As we move on there is an overwhelming sense of hills, space and water.

We are passing a closed station by Ardmore Distillery (Teachers): it seems strange that a station next to a distillery couldn't survive. The track here is jointed rail but is still a quick and comfortable ride. I notice another closed station with a forlorn and forgotten air (Gartly) before we arrive at Huntly; it is obvious that this has been a railway town of no little importance in the past, and although there is still a goods yard and buildings there are also many spaces where other lines once ran. The station building is very attractive but obviously not original.

On the left shortly after leaving the station, and situated in a beautiful setting beside the River Deveron, is Huntly Castle, built for the Gordon family in the sixteenth and seventeenth centuries. The line from Huntly is now downhill and the River Deveron is flowing like rapids with tumbling brown water and white horses. There are also fields with grazing horses and ponies; they are all wearing coats! The train is running very slowly here as repairs are going on to the embankment that has been dislodged by all the rain.

We are nearly at Keith and alongside the railway there are mountains of stored whisky casks waiting for the precious fluid and these are followed by rows and rows of huge black sheds which are presumably full of whisky.

Keith is another town that is a shadow of its former railway self and there is evidence that at one time there was a considerable amount of track work around the station. There is a large building with 'Chivas Bros' on it: it must be where Chivas Regal whisky is produced and stored.

Keith Station used to be known as Keith Junction to distinguish it from Keith Town on the former Speyside line to Elgin. The line from Keith (Town) is a wonderful survival story and the 11 miles to Dufftown is operated by the Keith & Dufftown Railway, which hopes to restore the rail link between the two Keith stations.

Just after Keith we pass Glentauchers Distillery, with a closed station (Tauchers Platform) next to it. Two young boys and a girl, all about 13, have just joined us. They have bought tickets from Keith to Elgin although they are travelling to Huntly, which is in the opposite direction. They say that they would rather pay the extra fare and be in a warm train than in the cold on Keith station. Timing is crucial to their plan as our train is due at Elgin just two minutes before their train leaves there, going in the opposite direction. It is already at the platform when we arrive and they rush across the bridge. They are only just in time, although I get the impression that they have done it many times before; it is a testament to the timekeeping of Scotrail.

The line crosses the River Spey and is now climbing through an area where there is much forestry, although my overall impression of the journey so far is of desolate moors and hills, all with a wild beauty of their own.

My first sighting of Elgin is of a huge Asda, a Currys, a Walkers Shortbread factory and other large stores. It is quite a culture shock, but then why should it be? People in Elgin need supermarkets just as much as anybody else. Although I won't see it today, Elgin has the superb remains of a beautiful and world famous thirteenth-century cathedral which is situated to the north of the station. Elgin's present station is not the original of 1902 which resembles a Scottish baron's home on a grand scale with its long frontage, upper storeys and conical towered turret at the end of the west wing. The station originally housed the administrative offices of the Great North of Scotland Railway.

With the closure of other lines in the area in the 1960s it was decided, for operational reasons, to build a new station. There are those who consider that the old station could have been adapted to the new track layout, thus enabling the public to continue to enjoy the majesty of the large booking hall. With its high glass domed ceiling, polished floors and wood-panelled walls it must have been a pleasure just to stand there, in addition to the feeling of importance that each person passing through the front entrance must have felt.

It is about time to mention again that it is still raining hard.

I have just realised that people here don't just discard their litter (not on the trains that I have used, anyway); they will make the effort to take their litter to the appropriate bin between the seats, even when they are leaving the train! My experience of the cleanliness, timekeeping and comfort of Scottish trains, together with the helpfulness of their staff, is in marked contrast to that which I experienced in other areas.

The line moves on, past more closed stations, to Forres. Forres is an ancient Royal Burgh and some historians say that its foundations might have been laid down before the birth of Christ. It became a Royal Burgh in 1140 and there was a Royal Castle here from AD 900. Much of the town's medieval layout has been preserved. The signal box is a delightful example from the Highland Railway although the station itself is a bleak-looking place with a very long platform. The station was originally the terminus of the line that ran from Aviemore through Grantown-on-Spey West and over the top at Dava to Forres.

Leaving Forres we cross the River Findhorn over a very high and enclosed wrought iron bridge; it reminds me a little of the tubular bridge at Conwy, and also the one that used to cross the Menai Straits before being burnt down in 1970. We are passing a castle on the right (I later find that it is Brodie Castle – sixteenth-century) and a small hill on the other side called Macbeth's Hillock. This is said to be the 'blasted heath' where Macbeth came upon the witches.

We are now in Nairn station. It is very picturesque, being freshly painted and with lots of flowers. It is also an opportunity to catch my first glimpse of the Moray Firth. The impressive Highland Railway stone building dates from 1885 and Nairn itself is a very Victorian seaside resort with an attractive front and views over the Moray Firth. As we leave Nairn I spot the floodlights of Nairn County FC. There is a lot of housing and industrial units close to the sea.

The rain is still coming down and we are now on what is almost an island with flooded land on each side of us. South of the line is Cawdor Castle, probably the most romantic castle in Scotland and home to the Thanes of Cawdor since 1370. It was linked to Macbeth by Shakespeare and its medieval tower and drawbridge are still intact. North of the line on the banks of the Moray Firth is Fort George. Following the Jacobite rebellion of 1745 and the defeat of Bonnie Prince Charlie at the Battle of Culloden Moor by the forces of the Duke of Cumberland in 1746, this artillery fortress was built (1748–69). Today it is unaltered and is a popular visitor attraction.

We have just passed another closed station. The view from the train is now of the Black Isle and the magnificent firth. I can also see the Kessock road bridge, with its tall spires, that forms the boundary between the Moray Firth and the Beauly Firth. The train is now passing underneath the line from Perth and we join it at Milburn Junction before entering Inverness.

Inverness is the capital of the Highlands and worthy of the title. As I get off the train I experience a sensation that I cannot put into words. There is a sense of having arrived somewhere very Scottish and very special, and it is a nice feeling to be here. I always have a similar feeling when I visit the Irish Republic – perhaps I have some Celtic blood in me. I know that this is just a railway station, but after Chester, Crewe, Glasgow, Stirling and Aberdeen it has a different feel to it. Perhaps it has something to do with its proud history and the men and engineers who created, against tremendous odds, the magnificence of the Highland Railway. I also think of William Wallace and Robert the Bruce, two mighty heroes who brought about, also against tremendous odds, independence for Scotland.

Inverness is a railway crossroads and I will have to pass through it three times. For that reason I have not made it one of my overnight stops, but thanks to leaving Aberdeen earlier than planned, I now have almost four hours here before my train leaves for Wick. I will also have two hours on the return leg from Wick.

On the station I am drawn to the WHSmith bookstall, initially to look for postcards until I spot a series of books which describe rail journeys in Scotland. They are an ideal companions for my travels and without any hesitation I purchase the Aberdeen–Inverness and Inverness–Perth editions. I ask the lady behind the counter if there are books in that series covering the lines to both Wick and Kyle of Lochalsh; she doesn't know but promises to find out for me, for when I return to Inverness in 24 hours' time.

Outside it is still pouring down with rain and although it is only early afternoon the station forecourt is lit up with lights which reflect from the wet tarmac. Across the street is Inverness Victorian Market and it draws me like a magnet. It was originally known as the 'New Market' and was built in 1870, and then rebuilt in 1890 after a fire. There are about 40 shops in it and they are all privately owned, none of your 'mass outlets' here! You can buy everything here from a postcard to full Scottish dress, together with toys, Beatrix Potter figurines, hardware, fruit, haggis and many other tempting things; you can even get a haircut! I manage to resist buying 'Hunka Munca', a kilt, a dirk and a haggis; there are probably very good reasons for not buying them but I am tempted. The Victorian Market is very conveniently situated in the centre of town and its entrance from Academy Street (opposite the station) has very attractive Corinthian stone arches, with animal carvings on the keystones.

The River Ness splits the town in two with the railway station and shopping centre to the east, with the High Street being linked to the west side of town by the Ness Bridge.

There are some very evocative street names such as Gordon Terrace, Argyle Terrace, Charles Street, Union Street and Celt Street. There are also some interesting ones such as Pancake Place and Raining's Stairs – appropriate today. Inverness Castle is situated close to the town centre and alongside the river. The castle dates from the twelfth century although Prince Charles's Jacobites blew up the Hanovarian fort in 1746. The present building dates from 1834 and is currently used as the Sherrif Court House.

I make my way to the Tourist Information Office which is very lavishly stocked with postcards, maps, videos, books, souvenirs, clothing, clan histories, interactive information points and even Internet stations. You can also book accommodation and tickets for special events. Nothing is too much trouble for the staff behind the counter.

My next stop is a shop selling everything Scottish and I nearly succumb to a clan tie pin. There is tartan, crystal and silver everywhere. There are many small side streets and interesting shops to explore, but I must go as time is running out. I make my way to the Eastgate Centre; this is a very new and very modern shopping centre and they are presently extending it alongside the railway line to house an additional 29 shops.

Back on the station I find two very interesting plaques on the platform wall which commemorate the completion of the line from Nairn to Keith in 1858, which in turn completed the rail link between London and Inverness. The plaques are from Joseph Mitchell's original box iron girder bridge over the River Spey between Keith and Elgin and were moved to Inverness when the bridge was rebuilt in 1906. One plaque lists all the directors of the Inverness & Aberdeen Joint Railway. The other plaque gives details about the contractors for the ironwork and masonry together with start and finish dates for the project, and an acknowledgement of engineer 'Joseph Mitchell F.R.S.E. Inverness'.

The plaques on Inverness station

Part of the wording on the first plaque is:

This railway extending from the town of Nairn to Keith, completing the communication between London and Inverness, was begun in October 1854 and opened to public traffic on 18th August 1858 and this viaduct crossing the Spey was completed in 20 months...

Feeling in need of a coffee I head for the refreshment room and, amazingly, the woman that was on the bus from Chester to Crewe is there! I manage to avoid her and while standing at the counter I hear her relating the story of 'a horrible Irish family' to someone who is obviously a local and a stranger to her.

It is getting towards darkness now and I will see very little of the journey to Wick, still four hours away. The train is very warm and comfortable and is full of people going home after work or a day's shopping. The atmosphere is relaxed and friendly and I settle back in my seat to enjoy the journey and perhaps catch up on my notes.

The train is now full but nobody is without a seat and I fall into conversation with the man opposite me. He is a student travelling home to Tain. He is 26 and studying Environmental Science at Inverness University. Although he was born in Edinburgh his parents moved to this area because of work and he now considers this area to be his home.

The first station out of Inverness is Beauly. This station has only just been reopened after closing 30 years ago, and it now has the smallest railway platform in Britain. Beauly is a very historic town and is set in an unspoilt area of mountains, lochs and forests and there are many examples of rare birds and animal life to be found in this area. Although it is wet and nearly dark you can still appreciate the beauty of the Beauly Firth and the view across towards Nairn.

Not long after Beauly is Muir of Ord, and the next stop will be Dingwall. The line from Inverness to Dingwall opened in June 1862 and in February 1894 Muir of Ord became a junction with the opening of a branch line to Fortrose.

As we enter Dingwall station my companion tells me that this is the home of Ross County FC who are able to muster a 3,000 attendance for their home games; there are many English lower-division teams who would be glad to emulate that. A sign on the outside of the football ground says: 'More than just a football club'.

As we pass through Alness he points out a group of very large standing stones on the top of a mountain in the distance. It is only just light enough to see them. There must be at least ten, each one about 30 or 40 feet high. He tells me that they are called The Firush (he pronounced it 'feerush') and says that they were built by soldiers returning from duty in India. The reason for this project was, apparently, to lift the morale of those returning soldiers who found no work when they returned home.

It is quite dark now and we have reached Tain where my companion gets off: it is a shame because he has been most interesting to talk to.

The train is now a moving island of light in the pitch darkness, with only the lights of an occasional station to break the view. My watch says that it is 7.30pm. It is two hours since we left Inverness and two hours more until we reach Wick. It is very comfortable and peaceful and the movement of the train is soothing.

I must have dozed off because it only seems a few minutes later and we have arrived at Georgemas Junction, I say 'must have dozed off' because it is just over 100 miles from Tain to Georgemas Junction; here the train reverses to make the journey to Thurso.

Everyone gets off except a couple sitting opposite me; they are father and daughter and have been to Inverness for a day out, shopping. They caught the 6.29 am from Wick this morning and I reflect that their day has included eight hours on the train. He is about 65 and a former railway employee who worked on this line. He remembers when the train stopped at all the stations from Inverness to Wick, about 60 of them (there are now 23). He recalls a slower and more gentle pace of life when the train stopped wherever someone needed a bucket of coal or a can of milk; he paints a very evocative picture of train travel before Beeching.

The train has now reversed again for the final leg from Thurso through to Wick. We pass through Georgemas Junction again and 15 minutes later we are at the top of Scotland, where the station board says: 'Welcome to Wick'.

It is 9.30 pm, very dark, very wet and deserted and I have no idea where my lodgings are situated. The situation is not as bad as it might seem however as the address is Harbour Quay, and as the road runs downhill alongside a river I conclude that it must end up somewhere by the harbour. As I walk downhill I can hear the rushing of the river alongside me, together with an occasional glimpse as the starlight is reflected on the water. The two other people from the train have been collected by car and have gone. Although it is only 9.30 pm, there is no traffic or people about and I plod my way downhill, alone in the rain.

At the harbour there is a big sea running and large rollers are forcing themselves against the downward flow of the river causing a maelstrom of confused water. Even in the half-light of the few street lights it is an impressive sight. My lodgings are easy to find as they are right on the front of the inner harbour.

The house is in darkness and I feel a slight qualm, which only increases as my knock is answered by a lady with an enquiring look. She is very apologetic and confirms that she had forgotten to log my booking, although she did remember our telephone conversation.

She does have a room though, and it is at the top of the house. It is spacious, clean, beautifully decorated and with every facility: coffee, TV, books, etc. etc. I choose the double bed (there is a single bed as well) which is extremely comfortable, and by 10.30 pm I am asleep!

I am awake at 5.45 am; it isn't raining and the wind has dropped quite a bit. The view is of an inner harbour with a few fishing boats, together

Wick – inner and outer harbour

with a John O'Groats tourist boat bobbing about on the relatively calm waters. Beyond that is a middle harbour and then an outer harbour. This gives an idea of the sort of seas that must hit this small town on the top of Scotland.

A cup of coffee and a leisurely shower and then I head for breakfast. The range of food that is available for breakfast is impressive and the bacon is the nicest that I have ever tasted. When I mention this to Brenda she says that virtually all the food that she serves is either grown or raised locally.

Bob and Brenda Turner, who run this establishment, share their home with their guests and the feeling of welcome is very warm. Bob works for Rolls-Royce in Thurso but used to be an engineer on a nuclear submarine (HMS *Superb*). There are pictures everywhere to do with his life in the navy and also some of trains and locomotives!

It's 9.30 and the sun has come out for the first time this week, although it is still very windy. I have just over two and a half hours before I move on, and I decide to explore the town and also visit the Caithness Glass factory. Brenda says that although they are going out I can leave my case for the morning, and she gives me a key to get back in again. This trust is both unexpected and pleasurable.

Wick town   Caithness Glass

Wick River   Wick from the hill

I call in at Woolworths to buy some postcards, only to find that they have been put away for the season! But, in keeping with everything else so far, it is no trouble to the assistant to go to the upstairs stock room to find them for me.

The Caithness Glass factory is on the Airport Industrial Estate about one and a half miles outside town. It is mostly uphill and I am glad that it has stopped raining. The factory sales area is like any up market shop in a big city and the range of goods for sale is impressive and glass sparkles everywhere. The airport is regional, and although you can charter a flight to Edinburgh, it will cost you £500!

I walk back into town and pause on the bridge that links the harbour and the rest of the town. The rich, dark brown-coloured river flows through the town to meet the sea in the harbour and it is very fast and wild-looking.

I cross the bridge and make my way to the monument on the hill that overlooks the old lifeboat station. There is a weak sun and the wind is still very strong but the view from up here is worth the walk. White and grey clouds race across the sky and across the bay I can see the town of Wick. There is a wild grey beauty about this place that I find irresistible. As I watch the sea crash against the harbour wall I reflect that this is the top of Scotland, where I have always wanted to travel to by rail, and out there is only the North Sea and the Norwegian Sea.

Wick is the most northerly town on the east coast of Britain and its origins go back to the Vikings, with the name of the town deriving from the Norse 'Vik', meaning a 'sea inlet'. The only remaining symbol of those days is the Castle of Oldwick known as the Old Man of Wick. It is a ruin perched on the clifftops immediately south of the town.

Wick became truly famous in the nineteenth century when local fishermen and merchants made it the largest herring fishing port in Europe, and at one time there were over 1,000 boats leaving its harbour every day. At Ulbister, just south of Wick, there is a lasting memorial to the fishing boom known as The Whaligoe Steps. These are 365 steps built into the cliff face in the mid-eighteenth century to link the clifftop curing station with the landing quay below. The local fisherwomen used to carry laden creels all the way up the steps to the cliff top and then walk the six miles to the markets in Wick. The fishing boom has long gone but there is still much to enjoy in this part of Scotland. The spectacular coastal scenery alone is worth the visit.

There are many other attractions, including museums, festivals, culture trails, castles, salmon fishing, bird watching, golf, markets and also the opportunity to see rare breeds of bird and animal that live in this part of Scotland.

The river through the town flows out of Loch Watten 10 miles away and this morning it is gently flowing to the sea, whereas just 14 hours ago it was a tumbling, rushing torrent of brown water.

Wick station this morning is bathed in weak sunshine. My time in the far north-east of Scotland was to be one of only a very few occasions that I saw the sun. Even in this remote little station at the top of Scotland, everything is spick and span, as always!

I am sorry to be leaving for it feels as if my whole effort so far this week has just been about getting to Wick rather than touring Scotland, and it therefore seems a shame to be leaving so soon.

The train pulls out dead on time at 12.09. There are very few passengers but this line is as much about serving the communities along it as getting from one terminus to another.

The view from the window is of a wild, wet and bleak countryside and it has started raining. There are virtually no trees and as the line follows

Time to go

Wick River it is not always possible to be sure which is the river and which is a flooded field. The noise of the jointed rails is very soothing.

We pull into Georgemas Junction. Nobody gets on or off and although the station has been refurbished to a certain extent, its only passenger function now seems to be as a junction where the trains from Inverness arrive and then reverse for the journey to Thurso before proceeding to Wick. There are sidings, and I can see some supermarket container traffic; it is good to know that some freight still goes by rail. There is a large lorry parked behind the station building and it is a moment or two before I realise what is different about it: it has been adapted to run on rails as well as road. It is a bleak and empty spot and I try to think why the original builders didn't make the junction at the town of Halkirk a mile and a half away, particularly as the line passes very close to it on its return to Inverness.

The man who was in charge of the refreshment trolley on last night's train is now on this one. He is a local man from Wick and he has brought his ten-year-old daughter with him to help. She is quite excited by the prospect and it undoubtedly adds a nice informal and friendly touch to the service. Can't see it happening on the Inter-city services though!

We have just crossed to the west of the River Thurso over what must be the original iron girder bridge; there is water lying everywhere. On the left I can see a church built like a castle, with turrets and battlements, I am not sure, but it might be in the village of Glengolly. All the sheep in the fields have 'sticky-up' ears that makes them look both alert and comical.

We are very nearly in Thurso and I can see a large graveyard with very tall tombstones: it is immaculately kept and is constructed in tiers leading down to the banks of a river. It is very picturesque.

At Thurso station there is a large area of covered cattle pens alongside the station and there are many cows inside making their presence felt. The station is busy and a lot of people get on and off the train. There is no apparent urgency and people are just standing around on the platform enjoying the brief sunshine, or getting on and off the train to talk to people that they know. Thurso is the most northerly town on the Scottish mainland and was founded over ten centuries ago by Viking Earls. In the ancient Norse tongue it was Torsaa (Thor's river). It became a boom town in the eighteenth century when flagstones from the surrounding quarries were used to make pavements before the days of concrete slabs and, as the town grew, a local politician, chronicler and inspired town planner decided that Thurso needed a new town extension. He was Sir John Sinclair and he laid out an attractive and effective grid pattern, and today his name lives on in the square of his name in the centre of town.

Thurso started to boom again from the late 1950s when the experimental Dome of Discovery was built at nearby Dounreay. This was part of the nuclear power programme of that time, and was a plan to research and develop fast reactor technology. At the present time the site is being decommissioned alongside an environmental restoration project. Despite this, Dounreay is still the biggest employer in the far north and there is also a visitor centre where you can see past work and future plans.

The harbour at nearby Scrabster is the departure point for the daily ferries to the Orkney Islands. In both the First and Second World Wars, Thurso, Scrabster and the railway all played an important role with troop-carrying trains from the south taking sailors, soldiers and airmen to Thurso and Scrabster for ferrying to the Scapa Flow naval base in Orkney. When the battleship HMS *Royal Oak* was torpedoed in Scapa Flow in October 1939, the survivors were ferried to Thurso.

The train has retraced its route to Georgemas Junction and we are now heading in a south-westerly direction to Inverness. The refreshment trolley is back again and I have the urge to eat; this always happens when I travel by train. The unofficial assistant is very excited and I think Father may be regretting his decision to bring her along. She is very sweet though.

We are passing through Scotscalder, the sky is a vivid blue and there is a vivid blue lake. There is mile after mile of bright brown heather on one side and forestry on the other.

The view at Altnabreac is just as good: there is a mountain covered in snow and with the bright sunshine glistening on it and the bright blue sky it feels a privilege just to sit and enjoy it.

The next station is Forsinard and here there is a RSPB nature reserve. There is also a petrol station which consists of two pumps in the grass verge, and two houses, one of which must be a shop, and there is nothing else. With the snowy mountains, the brown heather and the sunshine it is beautiful. There is another mountain covered with snow so that it looks like a gigantic white pyramid.

The 22 miles from Georgemas Junction to this point has been through a central area of the highlands totally unspoilt by man or anything else. There have been virtually no roads and only some isolated dwellings along the way.

The line now turns due south and will follow the A897 to Helmsdale on the coast. It would be interesting to find out why the builders of the line did not follow the perhaps more obvious route to Wick along the populated south coast of Caithness rather than the isolated route that they took. We have just passed Loch an Ruathair and have reached Kinbrace: there is not a lot here but the station house has made a beautiful private home.

On the right now is Kinbrace Burn, lots of brown tumbling water and a man fishing with his daughter; the train driver toots his horn and they both turn. The girl is about 12 or 13 and has long hair ruffled by the wind; she smiles and waves in delight and the man raises his fishing rod in acknowledgement. It is a lovely moment and reminds me of more leisurely times. I hope that I can, at least in part, transfer that moment to paper.

In the distance I can see the Maiden's Pap, with its covering of snow. Between the railway and the road is the River Helmsdale, and as we pass through Kildonan, there are raging rapids and a patient cormorant. There is a very precarious-looking footbridge over the river, suspended by ropes!

We are getting near to Helmsdale and are passing what appears to be a concrete salmon leap. There is a bridge spanning a cleft in the hillside and from under it there is a torrent of water pouring out and cascading down the hillside; it reminds me of a giant's mouth.

The ground is getting a little flatter and we are passing a field. In the middle of it I can see a Jaguar car! There are no houses, farms or tracks in sight and it appears to have been abandoned; what makes it appear incongruous is that the car looks to be in showroom condition!

The line has now turned east and we are at Helmsdale, a seaside town and from here we will pretty much follow the coast back to Inverness. I can see big rollers with the sun gleaming on them and the effect is pretty spectacular. There are a lot of pretty white houses on the hillside opposite the sea. It is still a beautiful day but the sky looks very dark and threatening ahead.

The line is now close to the sea and on the other side and we have just passed Brora station. The old Highland Railway has left its mark on this little station in the form of an engraving on one wall of the station building. It reads: 'H.R. 1895'. In keeping with most of the towns in this part of Scotland there is a golf course. Brora is a beautiful village and in addition to golf there is a Heritage Centre displaying artefacts and archaeology of the area.

The line is now on the land side of the road and we are passing through Dunrobin Castle station which is set in an attractive wooded area. We don't stop, but I can see that the entrance to the castle of the same name is right opposite the station. Dunrobin Castle is the home of the Clan

Sutherland and is the largest house in the Northern Highlands with 189 rooms. It is also one of Britain's oldest continually inhabited houses and dates from circa 1400.

As we leave Dunrobin, we pass over Golspie Burn and frighten a flock of wild ducks into flight; there must be at least 40 of them. On the left is Dornoch Firth and ahead is Loch Fleet; at the top of the loch the line turns north towards Rogart. ('Firth' means an estuary, from the old Norse 'fforthr' – fjord). We are passing through some very isolated countryside with swollen rivers on either side; the remoteness continues to be very beautiful.

Rogart station is very attractive and could almost be in a time warp. Like Brora, the wall of the station building has 'H.R. 1895' engraved on it. In addition, the small signal box still has a British Railways plate on it and together with an original tin Bryant & May advert there is also an original porter's trolley. The whole scene is like something from 40 years ago, and is nice to look at.

The view of the countryside continues unchanged with sheep and occasional isolated farmhouses. As the line turns south again at Lairg I can see sidings with tankers and it seems to be some sort of fuel depot. The community of Lairg is a little way from the station and lies at the southern end of Loch Shin, a large Loch some 20 miles long.

We are just passing the Falls of Shin before Invershin station. There is a magnificent waterfall here and it is one of the most exciting natural sights in the highlands, particularly in the summer when the salmon leap up the rocks on their way to the spawning grounds. The whole area is set in a wooded valley with a river running through it.

We have passed Culrain without stopping and are running along the shore of the Kyle of Sutherland towards Ardgay. There is snow on the mountains here and the ones that I can see are probably Carn Bhren (2,080 feet), and Carn Chuinneag (2,749 feet).

Ardgay is situated at the northern end of Dornoch Firth and the view is breathtaking. There are trees that grow down to the edge of a large brown lake and their leaves are multicoloured for autumn. There is a heron standing motionless on a small island in the middle of the lake.

The line continues to follow the shore of the firth and we pass yet another whisky distillery (I later find out that it is Glenmorangie) just before Tain.

Sadly, Tain station building, although open, is boarded up and looks a little forlorn. Amazingly, it still has its original station clock set in the wall, unfortunately minus its hands. Tain is set in a little bay of the Dornoch

Firth and in medieval times was a pilgrim centre. There is still a medieval church in a beautiful churchyard setting.

We have just passed through Fearn (without stopping) and are running along the northern shore of Cromarty Firth. On the other side of the firth is the Black Isle which has many attractions, including the opportunity to see dolphins, seals and red kites. Also on the Black Isle is the town of Cromarty, birthplace of Hugh Miller, eminent geologist, editor and writer. Cromarty is also the Highlands' best-preserved eighteenth-century town.

I can see six oil rigs moored close to the shore and at this distance they appear huge. Whether they are in for servicing, repair or mothballing, I cannot tell. They are opposite a closed station – Delny, just before Invergordon. There is not much remarkable about Invergordon station except that it too has its original station clock and it is in better condition than the one at Tain. I can see two more oil rigs, this time moored very close to the shore and at this distance they look like giant monsters rising out of the sea.

We pass Alness and Evanton (closed) until we reach Dingwall, the junction where trains from Inverness to Kyle of Lochalsh part company from the Wick line, which is what I will be doing in about two and a half hours' time!

We pass another closed station (Canon Bridge) and reach Muir of Ord. The waiting room on our side of the platform is of the bus shelter type and I am surprised to see graffiti on it: it is the first that I have seen in Scotland so far this week.

Muir of Ord has a distillery (Glen Ord), famous for its malt whisky. There is also an excellent 18-hole golf course which was established in 1875. It also used to be a junction after a branch line was opened from here to Fortrose in1894.

There is a lot of snow on the hills between here and Beauly. The line continues along the south shore of the Beauly Firth before slowing to an almost walking pace as it reaches Clachnaharry swing-bridge on the outskirts of Inverness: this wonderful contraption enables pleasure boats and fishing boats to access the Beauly Firth from the Caledonian Canal. It is operated manually and takes several minutes to complete the operation and until 1913 there was also a station here.

We are on time into Inverness. I have just less than two hours in Inverness this time and my first call is at WHSmith bookstall to see if they have any news of the other railway books that I asked about 24 hours ago. The shop assistant who helped me last time is on duty, her name is Sheila. She tells me that she has emailed and telephoned their wholesalers, other

The Caledonian Canal at Clachnaharry

branches of WHSmith and the publishers, all without success. Sheila thinks that they may be publishing the Inverness–Wick edition in the near future and says that if I leave my home number she will contact me and let me know. Three days after I return home she telephones me to say that there is as yet no publishing date but when she has one she will ring me again – what service! I must write to WHSmiths and tell them.

The 18.00 Inverness–Kyle train is the last of the day and as it may be quite crowded I decide to be the first to form the queue at the barrier. It is also a good spot to just stand and watch.

A gentleman walks by in full Scottish dress: jacket, waistcoat, socks, kilt, sporran, dirk, gleaming shoes, the lot. He is a most impressive sight and strides across the station hall with supreme confidence.

There is a girl of about 14 sitting on a circular wrought iron seat; she is eating crisps with the intensity of someone who has been set a task that must be completed as soon as possible. The movement of her hand from bag to mouth is continuous and she consumes four packets without a pause.

There is continual movement of people to and from the platforms. During the hour and a half that I am waiting, three trains arrive, two from Edinburgh and one from Aberdeen. There is still trouble with flooding on the Aberdeen line and the noticeboard says that a bus service is in operation for part of the way. There are also three departures: Aberdeen, Glasgow and Wick. All the trains are busy. Despite the numbers of people catching and leaving trains, there is none of the frantic haste and jostle associated with most main line stations south of the border.

It is time to join my train, which is pretty full, but the queue system at Inverness means that I have a good choice of where to sit and I settle back and make myself comfortable in a window seat.

We leave on time and the train retraces the route that I have just covered, but only as far as Dingwall, where it now branches off for Kyle of Lochalsh. The line from Dingwall to Stromeferry was opened in August 1870. The final ten miles from Stromeferry to Kyle was completed on 2nd November 1897 at a cost of £20,000 per mile and included some 31 rock cuttings and 29 bridges.

The train is warm and comfortable and moves at a leisurely pace. At each island of light that is a station, some people get on but mostly they are getting off. This line is not just a ride through beautiful countryside but is also a vital transport link between the east and west coasts of Scotland at this point, and Beeching's proposal to close this link in 1963 seems incomprehensible. The line was saved, but was again under threat in 1970 before it was reprieved after a vigorous campaign. The Scottish Chamber Orchestra ran a steam excursion to Kyle in 1982, playing as they went.

Sitting across from me are a young family; the parents are in their late twenties with a little girl of eight and a boy of about five. They are obviously a very close family and chatter continually all the way from Inverness to Kyle. The little girl is constantly asking her mother questions and she replies to them all with endless patience. The father reads stories to the little boy; he is a very good reader and uses emphasis, changes of tone and exclamations to make the stories more exciting and the little boy occasionally shouts with pleasure. The whole scene is very warming and the entire conversation and story-telling is carried out in Gaelic. Try as I might I am unable to identify any of the words used, although some of the pronunciation is similar to Welsh.

We have arrived in Kyle. The only passengers to get off are two elderly ladies, a middle-aged man, the family and myself. I follow the family up the ramp to the main road. The only directions that I have are the name of the house and that it is in Main Street, which is the road to Plockton. There is now nobody to ask and I flip a mental coin and turn left. Almost immediately I see a sign indicating Plockton and I trudge up that road in the rain thinking how far and how long ago it was that I was in Wick; it is actually only just over eight hours ago! Mrs Murchison had said that it was 'just a way up the road' and that there would be a board and a light on. As I climb the hill and leave the town behind I begin to wonder if there are two roads to Plockton but I am comforted slightly by the fact that there are still houses on my left. I suddenly see a police station and decide to ask if they know where the house is. It is, of course, shut but there is a light on and a place to shelter while I telephone Mrs Murchison to ask where her house is, but she is on the telephone! She is on the phone

100

for ages and I decide to carry on walking. This is partly to keep warm and partly because I am sure that I look suspicious sitting outside a closed police station and that it would therefore only be a matter of time before some patrolling bobby ran me in.

I am now about a mile outside town and am considering returning there and booking in at the hotel, but I keep on ringing. Eventually I get through to my hostess and she comes out to meet me; she is apologetic because she forgot to put the light on and had taken her B&B board down for the season! She is however a very nice, late middle-aged lady and insists on giving me home-made lemon cake and coffee; both are very welcome. The house is a bit like a moment frozen in time from the 1950s as the furniture, fittings and facilities are nearly all from that era. It is, however, very warm and comfortable and Mrs Murchison is welcoming and keen to know whether I have everything I want, including perhaps another piece of lemon cake? Coffee and an early night is all that I need at the moment.

The electrical arrangements in my room are somewhat disconcerting. When I eventually find the kettle hidden behind a curtain, I also find a forest of wires and follow them to a plug. In the plug there is a double socket which serves an electric blanket and a lead to an extension. The extension serves the kettle, a radio, a bedside light and a further extension! This extension serves two further lights on the dressing table and a piece of equipment, the use of which I am not sure. I decide to disconnect everything except the bedside light and kettle.

I wake up with a very sore throat. I am sure that I will either lose my voice or get a terrible cold, or both.

The breakfast is very nice and my hostess also gives me a magazine containing information about places and events in the area. She tells me that she has felt the financial pinch a little since the new Skye Bridge opened because fewer cars now stop in Kyle since the ferry stopped operating. I am glad that I didn't give up on her last night, and I bid her farewell.

It is a beautiful morning and as I walk down the hill to the town I can see the snow-covered mountains of Skye over the rooftops of the houses. There doesn't seem to be much of Kyle but what I can see is centred around a crossroads close to the loch's edge. Fortunately there is a pharmacy, which is open, and the lady behind the counter, who is the owner, is both sympathetic and helpful. She is from Kent and I ask how she comes to be in Kyle of Lochalsh. She tells me that her husband came up here with work, and they just stayed. They love the area, but integration has been a very slow process for them.

I ask her why there was, and is, so much opposition to the tolls on the new Skye Bridge, particularly as they would have had to pay on the ferry anyway before the bridge was built. It appears that the campaign against the bridge tolls is led by a group who, for one reason or another, had not had to pay the ferry tolls. It seems that this is a delicate matter for my confidante, so I don't press the subject.

The weather at the moment is quite superb with sunshine and fluffy white clouds and I walk around the corner to a circular car park raised above the level of the loch, and from here the outlook is really something. The mountains of Skye are a vivid brown and green with a thick cap of

The Cullins and Skye Bridge from Kyle

snow and the loch is a vivid blue with the white Skye Bridge in the background. The white houses and the Lochalsh Hotel sparkle in the sun. It is a view that you can drink in like a parched man would drink water. I feel that I can't get enough of it.

The first car of the day arrives on the car park and following a polite 'Good morning', I fall into conversation with the driver.

He has a holiday home in the area and has been coming here for years, and he is impressed with the convenience of the new bridge to Skye. We go on to talk about ferries that we have taken our car on, some of which have seemed like no more than a floating piece of wood, with an engine. We both particularly remember the ferry from Dunoon to Gourock.

There is a nice little cafe nearby, behind the Tourist Information Office, and I fancy a cup of coffee. The scones look delicious and I put aside the fact that it is only about an hour and a half since I had my breakfast. They are delicious, but my view is not shared by a man at a nearby table who suddenly complains very loudly that his is stale and must have been on display for some days; he is quite belligerent, but the waitress keeps her cool superbly. The replacement scone is apparently OK.

Before the Skye Bridge opened, there were two ferries shuttling back and forth on the five-minute crossing between Kyle and the village of Kyleakin. Now that the ferry service no longer runs, Kyleakin is a peaceful and pleasant little fishing village but with good facilities such as B&B accommodation, hotels, eating places and bars.

I feel a great reluctance to leave the Kyle of Lochalsh but it is time to move on once more and head for Perth, which some people have told me is a dour but interesting town.

Leaving Kyle

The train is on time, again, and as soon as it leaves the station it enters a deep cutting and then suddenly there is Loch Carron on my left. Another cutting and then we are following the curves of the loch first one way and then another, with the wheels screeching. Looking back I can now see the end view of the Skye Bridge. The hump of the main piece is so pronounced that you cannot see the other side!

Before it reaches Skye, the bridge has a landfall on an island called Eilean Ban. Gavin Maxwell of *Ring of Bright Water* fame once lived in a lighthouse keeper's cottage on the island; there is also a lighthouse on Eilean Ban which was designed by William Telford but is now no longer used.

The line continues to twist and turn as it follows the contours of the loch and we have now reached Duirinish station. In a field close by I can see Highland cattle for the first (and on this trip only) time. They look just like the ones on the postcards that you buy.

Plockton from the train is just like the postcards too, but with the added bonus of snow-covered mountains as a backdrop. The station is very pretty as well. Plockton is a very peaceful village and is in a sheltered bay that is warmed by the Gulf Stream. The main street is lined with palm trees and beautiful shrubs and it is a popular spot with visitors. It also has television fame, being the place where the BBC television series *Hamish MacBeth* was filmed. This was a comedy drama about a Highland bobby with a difference.

There are opportunities to see all sorts of wildlife in this area including seals, roe deer, pine martens, merlin, golden eagles, and tawny owls.

Across the bay from Plockton is Duncraig Castle, formerly the home of the Matheson family and latterly a college of further education. There is also a station at Duncraig.

The line is still following the shores of this very long loch and we are travelling at a very sedate speed. I can see an island with a pretty white house on it; it looks an idyllic place to live. Looking back I can see that the line is 'wedged in' between high cliffs and the loch; this must have been some construction job, no wonder it took so long to complete the section from Stromeferry to Kyle. You can see that there was nowhere else to put the line.

Stromeferry station still shows the evidence of once being a more important station than it is now. As I have already mentioned, it was the terminus of the line from Dingwall from 1870 to 1897.

I can see a black and custard-coloured trawler making its measured way down the loch towards Kyle.

The next stop is Attadale and I can see a motionless heron at the edge of the water. He suddenly takes off and follows us for a short while; he is very graceful and his slow and languid flight appears effortless.

About five miles south of Stromeferry is Eilean Donan Castle on the shore of Loch Alsh. It is the ancestral home of the MacKenzies of Kintail and dates from the thirteenth century, though later restored.

About two miles beyond Attadale, the loch suddenly becomes a river and then we are in Strathcarron station. This is a passing place for trains and there is one waiting to proceed to Kyle; passengers in each train stare at each other like fish in a tank.

The journey quickens as we are no longer following the loch. From deep clefts in a hillside there are cascading burns falling to the river below.

We have reached Achnashellach and must be higher here as the snow-covered mountains are quite close; as we leave the station the snow comes right down to the railway.

Suddenly, in the midst of nowhere, there is a magnificent grey house with many chimneys, standing proudly on the hillside with no apparent means of access (a later look at the map shows that there is a road, but it is not obvious from the train). It is a lovely spot and must look just as good in the summertime.

We are now totally surrounded by snow and the mountains, which are very close, sparkle in the sun and are breathtaking to look at. A few minutes later I look back and can see that we have just passed through a narrow winding pass completely snow covered. What a job building this line in winter!

Shortly after leaving Achnashellach the line crosses the road and we pass through Glencarron towards Loch Sgamhain. My carriage is virtually empty and I have been so absorbed by the view that I had completely forgotten that I have a camera! As I look back out of the carriage window I can see the snow-covered Torridon Peaks; I hope that my picture does them some justice.

We are just arriving at Achnasheen station and it is like most others on this line, in a very rural area but nevertheless an impressive building. Achnasheen is almost the halfway point between Kyle and Dingwall and has always been one of the major passing points on the line. It opened on 19th August 1870 under the auspices of the Dingwall & Skye Railway.

The view is still beautiful but the snow is now farther away from the train. Suddenly, across a panorama of brown and green heather there are the twin peaks of a mountain. Its tops are covered in snow that gleams in the sunlight and it is all the more visually pleasing because of the surrounding contrast colours. From a later study of the map it must be Scuir Vuillin (2,844 feet).

We have just passed through Achanalt. This is a very remote area and the station is situated alongside a loch of the same name, and to the east of Corriemoille summit. To the north there are only mountains and Loch Fannich. The station is a request stop only and has a slightly desolate air

Scuir Vuillin

despite its electricity and new name signs. The original station building has now become a private dwelling and only a small shelter is available for any waiting passenger.

Three or four miles later and we are at Lochluichart station which is on the edge of Loch Luichart, a very pretty location. As we leave Lochuichart, I reflect on the remote beauty that we have travelled through and the fact that although we have been following a road for the last 36 miles since we left Stromeferry I have only seen three cars!

The road that we have followed for so long is now joined by the one from Ullapool and we are running into Garve. Royal Assent was granted in August 1890 for a branch line from Garve to Ullapool but the plans were abandoned exactly three years later in August 1893.

The area is less rugged now and there are green fields and lots of trees and as we pass Loch Garve and swing away from the road towards Achterneed (closed 1964) we pass the point where, a little to the south, are the Rogie Falls.

We have just joined the Inverness to Wick line and are now running into Dingwall. The first railway reached Dingwall in 1862 when the Dingwall & Skye Railway opened. The company had originally planned to build the line to the west of Dingwall through Strathpeffer, because of easier terrain, but because of fierce opposition by landowners in that area they were forced to make a detour around the town. This was to prove Strathpeffer's loss, for although a branch line was later opened from Dingwall in June 1885, it was closed in 1951. The distance from Dingwall to Kyle is 63 miles and it must be one of the most scenic routes in Britain.

We have just crossed a bridge by Ross County FC when it suddenly occurs to me that this is the first train since I arrived in Scotland on which they have not announced the stations along the line. It also occurs to me that I have already passed this way three times in the last two days!

There is snow on the hills as we reach Muir of Ord. It is a very ordinary-looking station with the original buildings long gone and a graffiti-covered bus shelter-type waiting room in their place (this was to be the only graffiti that I saw in Scotland). The station was once Muir of Ord Junction where you changed for the Black Isle Line to Fortrose. That branch line opened in 1894 and closed to passengers in 1951, although it retained freight services until 1960.

The Black Isle is surrounded on three sides by the Beauly, Cromarty and Moray Firths and it is an area of much beauty and interest. It is also surrounded on three sides by the railway between Nairn, Inverness, Dingwall and Invergordon.

106

We have now reached Beauly. There is a ruined priory here that was founded in 1230 and became a Cistercian home in about 1510. Mary Queen of Scots visited here in 1564 and it is said that Cromwell took the stone from the priory to build a fort in Inverness in 1650.

The station closed in 1960 but following its recent reopening is a shadow of its former self. The station building is still there but is now a private dwelling with the platform on that side long gone and the area overgrown with small trees and weeds. Passengers now board and alight on a platform that is only slightly longer than a coach length.

We are now running alongside the Beauly Firth and towards the outskirts of Inverness itself. There is an impression of water everywhere but it is not floods: it is the closeness of the Moray Firth, Beauly Firth and the Caledonian Canal that impacts on you.

There is a good view of the Kessock road bridge that divides the two firths and links Inverness with the Black Isle. We are now almost into Inverness and there are several supermarket containers in the sidings. I later find that that company used to send everything by rail; I cannot tell whether they are still used as they look derelict and forlorn with weed-covered tracks leading up to them.

Inverness station. The train that I am on is a through service from Kyle to Perth and we only have ten minutes here, just enough to have a last look at this station and reflect on the many trains that go in and out of it in a day. It is also a chance to stretch my legs before the next lap of my journey and my overnight stop in Perth.

Not long after we leave Inverness the train comes to a halt. Again the courtesy and communication from Scotrail comes into action as the guard announces that there is a points failure ahead and we will have to reverse back to Inverness. We then run 'wrong track' past the fault and rejoin our own line. The whole procedure takes about ten minutes.

A few miles out of Inverness and we are passing the site of Culloden Moor station (closed 1965). The closure of this station seems without reason to me for it is just a mile from the historic battlefield of the same name with its tremendous potential for future tourist development.

In my opinion, the railway closure programme of the early 1960s was quite wrong. The problem was seen and recognised by many as overmanning, not overcapacity, and the decimation of the railway system and subsequent underfunding by all governments meant that effective updating and development of the railway system was many times harder than it should have been.

There is a lot of speculation about the wholesale railway closure programme brought about by the Conservative Party but even the Labour Party reneged on its pre-election pledge in 1964 when it said that it would halt all major rail closures. Following their election victory of 1964 the closure programme, under Labour Transport Minister Tom Fraser, actually accelerated. How many people and train companies of today would like to have the infrastructure of the 1960s back? Most of them, I am sure. Enough, this is supposed to be a record of my journey around Scotland by train but the short-sightedness and ill reasoned decisions of the 1960s still make me, an ex-railway man, very angry.

There is a very high and impressive viaduct over the River Nairn just past the site of Culloden station. It is made of red sandstone and has many arches. The area here is now quite remote and there is plenty of snow as we pass through a cutting and the site of Daviot station (closed 1965). Daviot was where the Highland Railway obtained the granite for constructing the line. In contrast to the train, which is full of passengers, the view outside contains no human beings, only moorland, burns full of water, and forestry.

It is peacefully beautiful as we pass over Aultlaslanach viaduct at Moy. Moy Hall is the seat of the Clan Mackintosh, although the original was a castle built on an island in Loch Moy during the fourteenth century. Moy station, although closed, is still there and is now a private dwelling. Lloyd George and George V once used the private waiting room of the Mackintoshes at this station.

We have now just passed the whisky distillery at Tomatin and are crossing the Findhorn viaduct. You can't see the magnificence of the structure from the train but from photographs I know that it is a dramatic sight with its steel trusses supported by tapered masonry piers.

We are now climbing through a deep cutting to Slochd summit, 1,315 feet above sea level, and as we afterwards run downhill for the five miles to Carrbridge there is extensive forestry. The station here was originally known as Carr Bridge when it opened in 1892 and was only changed to Carrbridge by British Rail in 1983. The complete section of line from Aviemore to Inverness was opened in 1898.

We are now at Aviemore which is an extensive and busy station and there are a lot of passengers about for it is a very popular holiday centre and I can see lots of holiday chalets. It is also a very popular and well-known skiing resort, with the Cairngorms close by. The station was beautifully restored in 1998 and was the largest station on the Highland Railway, after Inverness. The first railway to reach Aviemore was the line from Boat of Garten in 1863.

There is a Black Five Locomotive waiting at an adjacent platform to take its train to Boat of Garten and Broomhill. This is the Strathspey Steam Railway that opened in 1978 following the closure in 1965 of the old Highland Railway that ran from Aviemore to Forres, Nairn and Inverness. From Boat of Garten another line, operated by the Great North of Scotland Railway, ran to Craigellachie and Elgin; this line also closed to passengers in 1965.

We have just passed the site of a closed station (Kincraig) and are running through a wild and bleak landscape with the snow-covered Cairngorms as a backdrop. Funny how I used to think that this would be a 'rambling' line; it is in fact an express route also served by GNER (the Great North Eastern Railway) and trains at this point are clocking nearly 100 miles an hour.

We have reached Kingussie station. It is an attractive building erected in 1894 to replace the original timber structure. There are not many passengers to get on or off although the station does serve a small town. In the distance on high ground I can see Ruthven Barracks that were fought over in the 1745 Jacobite Rebellion.

Just 3 miles further down the track is Newtonmore station. Although the station building survives, it is privately owned. There is a new single platform and bus shelter waiting room, although the old 'up' platform still exists. There is a museum at Newtonmore devoted to the story of the Clan Macpherson and its place in the history of Badenoch.

We have been following the River Spey since we left Aviemore but it now branches off to the west and its place is taken by the River Truim, which is itself a tributary of the Spey. Although I cannot see it, we have just passed the Falls of Truim where there is a good salmon leap during the autumn.

The scene here is quite bleak and there is a lot of snow on the surrounding hills as we run past Dalwhinnie Distillery (opened 1898) which, at 1,073 feet above sea level, is the highest distillery in Scotland. It reminds me that I still have some Dalwhinnie whisky at home, a present from my son some years ago.

The station at Dalwhinnie is still open but we do not stop and from here to Blair Atholl it is now double track. A couple of miles on and we have just crossed a viaduct over the River Garry and are now at the highest point on the line, Druimuachdar Summit at 1,484 feet above sea level.

Shortly after and we are passing the site of Dalnaspidal station (closed 1965). When it was open it was the highest station (1,405 feet above sea level) on a main line in Britain. In the days of steam, trains from Blair Atholl to Dalnaspidal would be double-headed or banked from the rear for the 17-mile-long gradient known as the Druimuachdar bank. The track now curves one way and then another as it winds down between the desolate ruggedness of the Grampian Mountains.

Blair Atholl, and the scenery is now much softer. In the days of steam there was a small loco shed here to service the station pilot and banking locomotives. It is an attractive and original little station with a timber signal cabin at the level crossing. Nearby is Blair Castle which has the only remaining private army in Europe, the Atholl Highlanders.

From Blair Atholl to Pitlochry (the next stop) is only seven miles but in-between we pass Killiecrankie station (closed 1965). It was to the north of Killiecrankie in 1689 that 'Bonnie Dundee' (Graham of Claverhouse) defeated the forces of William of Orange, although he lost his own life in the short fight.

Shortly after passing the site of the station we enter a small tunnel and then cross Killiecrankie viaduct before entering Pitlochry. The station is very attractive and there are a lot of passengers to get on.

We are now only 29 miles from Perth and this is my fifth consecutive day on the rails of Scotland. I feel as though I could do another five without any difficulty and there is a slight sadness that the trip is now nearing its end. I had intended to include Edinburgh – Glasgow – Oban – Fort William – Mallaig as well, but because of difficulties with the rail service in my home area I may have to travel home after a night in Perth. I will complete my Scottish journey at a later date.

Pitlochry is a delightful Victorian town full of charm and is a very popular place for tourists. It was the winner of 'Best Small Country Town' in the Britain in Bloom 2001 competition. It also has the smallest whisky distillery in Scotland – Edradour.

Away to the west are Loch Tummel, Loch Rannoch and Glengoulandie Deer Park. Rannoch Moor was made famous in R.L.Stevenson's *Kidnapped*. On the platform there is a cast iron drinking fountain that looks like a heron perched on a vase. Although no longer working it is very interesting to look at.

There is a sense of hustle and bustle on the platform but despite the urgency of people to get aboard and the train to leave, I risk leaving the train for a few moments to take some photographs. These are to show a colleague of mine at work, who holidays in Pitlochry frequently.

This is yet another train running to time and we leave promptly at 16.18. It was nice to see that although the line is served by express trains, the movements are still controlled by semaphore signals.

As we leave the station the colossal Atholl Palace Hotel dominates the view. It was opened in 1878 and was originally designed as a hydro-pathic establishment for the treatment of disorders, by the application of water.

The train is following the River Tummel and to the East, not far away, is Ben Vrackie (2,757 feet). As we pass through a belt of forestry we reach the site of Ballinluig station (closed 1965). Ballinluig was originally a three-platform junction with a 9-mile branch to Aberfeldy, which also closed in 1965. Amazingly, this branch had 41 bridges and many cuttings and embankments and today would have been, I am sure, a very profitable and beautiful tourist line.

Robert Burns was so entranced by the Falls of Moness at Aberfeldy during his Highland tour of 1787 that he composed one of his best-loved songs, 'The Birks o' Aberfeldie':

> Now simmer blinks on flowery braes
> And o'er the crystal streamlet plays
> Come let us spend the lightsome days
> In The Birks o' Aberfeldie.

Today there is no sign that Ballinluig or Aberfeldy stations ever existed.

There is more forestry and we then pass through Inver Tunnel and over Inver Viaduct, which crosses the River Braan, and into Dunkeld & Birnam station. The station is the original of 1856 and has imposing square stone chimneys and attractive ironwork under the station canopy. There is a latticework over-bridge connecting the two platforms and, again, trains are controlled by semaphore signals.

There is a Beatrix Potter exhibition by the station in a building used by her when she came on holiday there in 1892 when she was 26. The first stationmaster at Dunkeld was John Kinnard and it was he who organised the accommodation for Beatrix Potter for her holiday. The River Tay runs between Birnam and Dunkeld and the two towns are linked by the Telford Bridge. The whole area is extremely attractive.

About a mile after leaving Dunkeld and Birnam, we pass Rohallion Castle to the West and then Kingswood tunnel. Immediately south of the tunnel there used to be a private platform for the Laird of Rohallion Lodge but this was closed in 1864.

Another two miles down the line and we are passing the site of Murthly station (closed 1965). This was one of the many stations on this line to fall victim to the closures of the 1960s. Perthshire's County Asylum used to be situated adjacent to Murthly station and a siding ran into the grounds.

We are now only seven miles from Perth and passing the site of Stanley Junction Station. There is now nothing to indicate that there was once an important station here. There is only the single line heading north to Inverness and a signal box controlling the switch, at this point, from single track to double to Perth. Everything else has gone. Stanley had three platforms and was the point at which Caledonian Railway trains headed east through Forfar on their way to Aberdeen. This was in fact the original main route from Glasgow to Aberdeen but Stanley station closed in 1956. Forfar lost its passenger service in 1967 and the line east of Stanley closed completely in 1982.

Perth. Arriving here on a wet and dismal Thursday is a depressing experience. The platform is dark and forlorn and the only staff on duty appear to be two British Railway policemen. The whole area cries out for some nice platform furniture, a refreshment room, a newsagent, a coat of paint and some bright lighting. Even in daylight it is dark under the

Perth

112

forbidding-looking station roof. Beyond the protection of the roof the rain is still falling steadily. The two policemen are pleasant and helpful and a gentleman in the station manager's office is extremely helpful with train information. I did revise my opinion of Perth station the following day, but more of that later.

It is not totally clear which is the way out but I can see what appears to be a main road beyond the long car park and this turns out to be Glasgow Road, on which I want number 36, which is only about a quarter of a mile away. Clifton House is easy to find, with its impressive corner tower.

Very nice accommodation and I have a large en suite room big enough for four or five people. I am tired and wet but decide to have a meal before relaxing with a book and some coffee. Hotel/Pub up the road where I have haddock and chips for £6.75, very poor-quality meal but it was only thing on the menu that wasn't chicken!

I have started a cold or something with a runny nose and sore throat and this, together with problems with the rail service in my home area and a shortage of time, finally decides me to cut my visit short and head for home in the morning. I was due to stay in Dundee tomorrow night and then onward to Edinburgh via the Tay and Forth bridges and from there to Glasgow and up the west coast but it is a bit rushed and I will return and cover the missing sections of my rail tour of Scotland, more comprehensively, at another time. My cold would also very probably spoil what has been a wonderful rail experience around Scotland. All the trains have been on time, clean and comfortable. Also, all the Scotrail staff that I have met have been very pleasant and helpful, particularly the guard on the Aberdeen to Inverness train and the Perth office staff.

I can catch the 9.56 am *Highland Chieftain* from Inverness to Kings Cross arriving in Edinburgh at 11.23 with a connection to Crewe at 11.50. This will comfortably get me home in the late afternoon.

On an extremely wet Friday morning I try to take some photographs outside Perth station but it proves too difficult to shield the camera from the rain and take decent pictures at the same time. Perth is a vast junction station, but when I arrive at 8.50 am there is not a soul to be seen! The whole place is eerily quiet with no trains, no passengers and no staff. The extent of the station is quite bewildering and it seems to have been left in a time warp from the nineteenth century. The first of three footbridges that I cross was made by Alex Findlay & Co. of Motherwell in 1893 and the whole appearance of the place, despite its faded air, gives the impression that nothing has changed since then. The gloom and the silence give it an almost sepulchral feel. Despite all this, Perth station retains its grandiose effect and it is a pleasurable feeling to explore it.

The first footbridge leads to another deserted platform and when I cross the second one, the same thing is repeated. The third footbridge leads me to a tunnel and as I emerge I receive a culture shock. On two sides of a terrazzo floor there is a travel office, a refreshment bar and a newsagent, all from an era quite different from that which I have just left. The impression is that all these amenities have been hidden away by platform 2, but it turns out that this is the main entrance! The main entrance block to the station, while no doubt efficient, I would compare to a modern brick extension attached to an old castle.

I am back on the platform that I arrived on as it is from here that I

Perth station clock

will depart. Everything is still quiet and deserted and I take time to admire the lovely old clock next to the station manager's office. It was made by J.A. Ritchie & Son of Edinburgh.

The *Highland Chieftain* arrives at Perth spot on time and suddenly, as if from nowhere, about 20 passengers for this train appear; the place seems positively crowded! As we pull out of the station it is still raining but now with some snow mixed in it.

The run from Perth to Edinburgh, via Stirling, will be the end of my rail trek around Scotland this time and although this part of the journey is not particularly interesting, my journey as a whole has been a truly memorable experience.

The *Highland Chieftain*

During the writing up of this journey I have referred to two maps of railways in Scotland; one is the current issue, the other is from 1954. It is very sad to see the demise of some of the lines, which today could well have been profitable in environmental, tourist and commercial terms.

3

Scotland 2007

Too much time has passed but I am now back in Scotland again and although it is the same month as when I was last here (October), the weather is quite different as the snow has not yet arrived and the sun is shining out of a blue sky with just a few lazy clouds drifting past.

Glasgow Central station does not seem to have changed much since I was last here and still has its great iron girdered roof with acres of glass. The Central Hotel within the station also still has its beautiful curved timber frontage and although the station itself, and the trains using it, have been changed to suit the twenty-first century there is still a timelessness about the place.

It is, however, rush hour and extremely busy, and if you stand in the same place for too long there is the risk of being knocked over by a passing parcel truck or even a desperate passenger rushing for his homeward-bound train.

Outside, Glasgow is as big and bustling as ever and the huge and impressive Victorian architecture towers above everything. There is plenty of time for the leisurely stroll to Queen Street station and the train to

The Tardis

A lone piper

117

Oban, and along the way I pass a lone piper entertaining the very cosmopolitan crowd that surges past him. Across the way there is an old-fashioned blue police box and is it not difficult to imagine Doctor Who stepping out of it at any moment to warn the crowd of some alien invasion.

Queen Street is still a clean and immaculate station and is also dealing with the hordes of rush hour commuters very efficiently. High above is a great domed glass roof and at the end is an arched glass frontage very similar to the one that used to be at Manchester Central station.

Queen Street station

I get into conversation with two British Transport policemen who are standing impassively watching the ebb and flow of people on the concourse; they tell me that despite the huge numbers of people using the station, crime here is not a significant problem. They are proud of their role in the Strathclyde Police and there is some good-natured banter and comparison between Scotland and North Wales.

There is something about rail travel that causes me to want to eat, and sitting here staring at a shop selling freshly made baguettes and rolls, the temptation was too much and I am now tucking into a large and crusty baguette filled with delicious tuna and mayonnaise; this is despite the fact that I am booked to have a meal on the train in about an hour or so.

It is a smooth ride out of Queen Street and although it is now nearing darkness it is easy to see the large warehouses with such names as Cutty Sark and Famous Grouse. There are also great stacks of wooden barrels. There are several stations out of Queen Street but these are served by the excellent Metro service and we only stop at Westerton and Dalmuir before Dumbarton; just after Dumbarton and beyond the Firth of Clyde and behind the hills there is a beautiful glowing sunset.

It is now quite dark and there are no distractions to be seen outside, which means that I can give my full attention to the excellent meal that is now being served at seat. There is a starter of smoked salmon salad which is followed by chicken breast wrapped in ham and served with pasta and salad. Wine is also available and the meal is concluded with some really nice cheese and coffee.

There are now 11 stations between here and Oban and each one appears and disappears out of the darkness like an island of light. It is a warm and comfortable journey and the three hours to Oban pass quickly.

From the station I can see high above the town the floodlit McCaig's Tower; it is an amphitheatre-like structure – but more of that later. Across from the station and dominating the waterfront is the Caledonian Hotel which is my base for the next few days; it is an impressive-looking building with a slightly nautical air and was originally built in 1882.

A very comfortable night is followed by an excellent breakfast with plenty of choice, and standing outside this morning at 7.30 am it promises to be a beautiful day. There is time for a short walk around the harbour area before the 9.40 am ferry across the Firth of Lorn to the Isle of Mull.

Naturally I head for the station first, and find that the new structure was erected in 1986. It replaced the original and impressive Victorian structure which was a very large affair with a great glass-domed roof covering several platforms and lines; it also boasted several facilities for the traveller and when it was demolished in 1985 it was to the dismay of many people. There is a plaque on Oban station celebrating the 125th anniversary of the completion of the Callander & Oban Railway, 1880 to 2005; the plaque also includes the name of 'R.N. John Anderson, 1837–1911', with the words: 'without whom the line would not have been completed'.

As the line leaves the station it curves away to the left and through a deep cutting with a backdrop of tree-covered hills dotted with a few houses in between the trees, it is a very attractive sight. There is a waterfront restaurant and a heritage wharf warehouse with a vast range of all things Scottish that you can buy. There is an impressive-looking boat tied up at the wharf; it is registered from Stornaway and the name on the side is *Hjalmar Ejorge*.

Oban as a town expanded greatly in the nineteenth century and although there is a lot of Victorian architecture it is not overpowering and the town has a style of its own. Despite the fact that it is a popular holiday town in the summer it has steadfastly refused to spoil its waterfront with amusement type arcades. As I stand waiting for the Caledonian MacBrayne ferry for Mull I look across the harbour at the town and it seems to sit here in its little space with the bay and the harbour and the hills, secure in its own surroundings, and you can imagine it changing very little over the years.

The trees on the hills that crowd in right to the edge of town are very much in their autumn splendour with gold and brown and green leaves, with the odd house perched impossibly on the edge of some of the cliffs. Peeping over the rooftops of the water front buildings I can also see the chimney of the Oban distillery which was established in 1794. Perhaps there will be time for a taste tomorrow.

The ferry to Mull

North Pier and McCaig's Tower from the ferry

Despite the fact that the sky is blue and the sun is shining there is a very brisk wind here on the top deck of the ferry. Looking down, past the smart new terminal, I can see the nearby area that used to be covered in a vast array of railway sidings in the days when there was a huge agricultural market and the train was the main source of transport. Before the First World War they used to run a train to Stirling for five shillings (25p) return. It was called the whist train as they used to play whist during the journey, followed by a day out in Stirling.

Despite the long procession of vehicles loading including a petrol tanker, a coach, cattle wagon, motor bike, cars and vans, they are soon stowed and we are on our way for the 40-minute crossing to the Isle of Mull.

The ferry pulls away from the quayside leaving a bubbling wake of water behind it as it crosses the bay that is sheltered by the island of Kerrera, where Alexander II of Scotland died in 1249, and into the Firth of Lorne. The views are special, with the mountains of Mull looming ever nearer and away on my right the island of Lismore in Loch Linnhe where I used to fish for sea trout many years ago. As Oban gets further away the impression of it fitting snugly into the surrounding mountains is very strong.

The sun is sparkling on the water as we reach the pier at Craignure and disembarking is a very simple process as there is just a short stroll along the pier to the road that runs through this very small place. It is composed of a Tourist Information Centre, a shop, a pub, a police station, a garage and a few houses, but more importantly today it is also home to Mull Rail, the first Scottish island passenger railway. It is a delightful little set-up and the 10$1/4$-inch gauge railway runs from Old Pier station at Craignure

Lady of the Isles – Mull Rail

Tarmstedt Halt – Mull Rail

Victoria – Mull Rail

121

through woodlands and along the coast for about one and a half miles to Torosay Castle.

There are two immaculate steam locomotives running today, and as the train with its little carriages with their wooden seats rattles through the woodland, the moss-covered trees almost reach to the line. In an open country section there is a little halt called Tarmstedt and an opportunity to take a photograph of the other train as it passes us. The views from here are spectacular, as across the Firth of Lorn are Ben Nevis, the Glencoe Hills, Lismore, Ben Cruachen, and up ahead I can see Duart Castle.

The terminus of the line is called Torosay and from here it is just a short walk through the woods to Torosay Castle which stands in 12 acres and is still home to the local laird, but with public admission to a lot of the rooms. It is an imposing grey stone Victorian country home, fronted with formal Italianate terraces from which I have just taken a picture of Duart Castle. This castle, also open to the public, is the ancient seat of the Clan Maclean and dates back to the thirteenth century; today it is the home of Sir Lachlan Maclean. It stands on a clifftop guarding the Sound of Mull and with its ancient cannons still pointing seaward, and beyond that the magnificent range of mountains on the mainland. It is truly a special place to be.

Torosay Castle   Duart Castle from Torosay

The rest of the gardens at Torosay include alpine beds, an oriental garden, a water garden and its famous statue walk. There is a cafe discreetly hidden at the side of the castle and I take my tea and biscuits to enjoy at a bench in the sun. I now find that the birds here are amazingly tame, as the bullfinches and chaffinches that abound actually come and feed from your hand.

Inside the house it is surprisingly warm and bright and it is interesting to browse through the family scrapbooks that are on view and detail the exploits of family members, relating to voyages around Cape Horn in a

'Eagle' on the front lawn

Beautiful bullfinches

square-rigger and escapes during World War Two. There are also lots of photographs and memorabilia from the same era.

We are now on a very attractive drive across Mull and are heading for Fionnphort where there is a short ferry crossing to Iona. There are just odd houses here and there, some of them with Scottish flags flying, and every so often little inlets of water, which turn out to be Loch Spelye and Loch Buie. There are broad vistas of mountains and rolling plains and bits of forestry; it reminds me a little of Snowdonia but perhaps more luxuriant. A hawk hangs motionless in the wind watching his prey in the grass below, while on the other side a burn cascades down the hill with the tumbling water sparkling in the sunlight.

We have just made a short stop at Pennyghael on the banks of a broad loch. There are only a few houses and the old smithy but it is an attractive place and the grassy area by the loch's edge is very inviting. There is a burn heading for the loch that has to pass under a very old and narrow stone bridge, and at this point we are at the extreme end of Loch Scridain.

Pennyghael

A bit further on and the loch has now widened out into the sea, and across the water I can see the island of Staffa where you can visit Fingal's Cave, immortalised by Mendelssohn in his overture to the Hebrides. As we near Fionnphort there are more houses and cottages but it is all relative and to me it seems a very isolated place to live.

We have arrived at Fionnphort and I am surprised to see just how close Iona is: it can't be more than a mile away. The ferry is quite a small affair and can only take about five or six cars and about 50 passengers. The sea

Fionnphort

The abbey on Iona

The chapel on Iona

Mull from the chapel

Inside the chapel

is quite choppy and there is a fair swell running: it makes the short crossing quite exhilarating.

Iona is a small island only about three miles long but is significant for being the birthplace of Christianity in Scotland and the abbey dominates the view as the ferry approaches the shore. There is a shop, restaurant and a few houses as you land and is then only a short walk to the abbey.

Adjacent to the abbey and set amongst ancient gravestones is St Oran's chapel, built in the twelfth century and the oldest of Iona's surviving ecclesiastic buildings. It was used as a chapel and burial place for the MacDonald family, lords of the Isles, and is a rough, stone-built place with a tiny window and a low doorway. Despite the simplicity of the inside it is full of atmosphere, and standing alone inside, it is difficult to imagine the people who have worshipped here and been buried here for the last 800 years.

Outside there are some sad stories in the graveyard, like the quarry manager and his wife who were both predeceased by an infant son, and then their daughter-in-law. There is a tall monument that says: 'A sailor of the 1939–45 war, merchant navy, was found 6th November 1940 and known only unto God'. There is a simple lichen-covered stone to mark the final resting place of the Duchess of Argyll who died in 1970, but a lot of the graves have no words and are just slabs of original stone.

If there is such a thing as a good spot to end up then this is quite something, looking across at the Isle of Mull with the wind-lashed waters in between and the mountains in the background. It is a place where sea eagles fly and the air is clean and fresh. It is also easy to imagine this place looking the same in another 800 years.

Back at the ferry point there is plenty of time for a look round the shop which has an extensive selection of goods from bread and milk to wet

Louise Morris Clews – Duchess of Argyll

weather gear and souvenirs. It is just starting to rain and the man on the till suddenly excuses himself to dash up the road to get his washing in – truly multitasking.

It is time for a wee dram of Tobermory, the whisky of Mull, in the warm sheltered surroundings of the bar-restaurant, and from its windows that look out across to Fionnphort I can see the ferry approaching. The swell is such that the name of Caledonian Macbrayne on the side of the boat briefly disappears as it heels over before the wind: this is the ferry that I have to take back.

Outside while I wait for the ferry I get into conversation with Gerry who lives in Fionnphort and works at the Abbey here. A long-term bus driver of 32 years, he gave it up because of cars driving too fast on the narrow roads of Mull. I mention the weather and he says that this is only a wee breeze, this despite the fact that it is blowing like hell. When I say that there is a large swell running he replies that it is no more than there is in his bath on a Saturday night.

There is a lovely white beach here and the water is crystal clear. We are under way and I am sure that the weather is trying to tell us that we should not be here, as in addition to the swell, there is a very strong wind and the white horses are chasing each other across the tops of the sea while the last rays of the sun are glistening on the heaving waves. The crossing is great fun.

On the way back to Craignure the road sweeps round the bottom of an inlet of Loch Scridain: here there is a place called Bunessan that snuggles in at the water's edge. There are a few fishing boats and with the sun glistening on the waters of the loch and the mountains, together with the Island of Staffa in the distance, it is a picture postcard scene.

Back at Craignure and there are a lot people disembarking from the incoming ferry, most of whom are laden with shopping. I suppose that with so few shops on Mull it is the obvious thing to do, stock up in Oban.

Seven o'clock and Mull is vanishing astern into the darkness. I get into conversation with the young lady in charge of the coffee bar who lives in Mallaig; she says that she goes to all the islands with her job but it is only for six months of the year. She spends the rest of the year travelling and has been to India, Laos and Thailand and says what a fantastic city Bangkok is but loves and prefers this part of the world. It is nice to hear her speak so enthusiastically about Scotland and its islands.

Early breakfast today as I am catching the 8.15 am train to Crianlarich where there is a change and another train to Fort William.

It is a grey, misty, murky morning as the train pulls out of the station.

The line gradually curves almost right around until we are above the town and there is a nice view of it and the harbour spread out below.

We have just reached Connel Ferry, the first station out of Oban; this was originally a junction where a 27-mile branch line that opened in 1903 ran to Ballachulish. For most of its length it followed the road and it is still possible to see most of the track bed on that journey. Connel Ferry eventually closed in 1966 and nothing remains of the original station area and through platforms. Today, there is only one platform and that is the one that used to be used by the branch line trains.

The countryside here is now very green and rural and the train has been running alongside Loch Etive. We have reached Taynuilt where there is a very neat and refurbished station with lots of sidings. After Taynuilt, and we are now running alongside a very deep valley and not long after the valley there is a beautiful lake: it is very grey and murky over the lake, the whole scene is misty, evocative, atmospheric and almost primeval.

At Loch Awe there is a coach on the old siding that serves as a cafe, and beyond it and across the water I can just make out Kilchourn Castle on its headland jutting into the loch. Loch Awe is long and narrow and stretches southward for about 30 miles. Just after the station the line crosses the river via the beautiful Orchy Viaduct. The station at Loch Awe was actually closed in 1965 but reopened in 1985.

The next station is Dalmally and here there is a magnificent backdrop of mountains, although with all the mist and cloud the view is not very good. Dalmally was originally the terminus of the Callender & Oban line from 1877 until the extension into Oban was completed in 1880.

We are nearly at Crianlarich and passing Tyndrum Lower there are many holiday cabins and caravans and a lot of forestry, and not much else to be seen.

Crianlarich, and the mist-covered mountains that are mostly covered in forestry, crowd in and seem to hang over the station. It is still an island platform although Oban and Fort William trains mostly use only one side. As there is a 30-minute wait for the Fort William train I opt for a hot cup of coffee in the little refreshment room that is decorated with photographs old and new of locomotives at work on the line.

I have memories of this station from many years ago of it being nearly buried in snow and the trains almost unable to get through. Today it is a constant fine drizzle that seems to penetrate everything and I am glad of my umbrella.

Sitting outside with a book and an umbrella I read about the time when two separate lines operated at Crianlarich, here the West Highland crossed

Misty Crianlarich   Towards Fort William (Oban line on the left)

over the Callander & Oban line and there were actually two stations here. There was also a link between the two, but this was just used for freight. It was only in 1965 after a rock fall just outside the station on the Oban line that those trains were rerouted permanently over the link line, thus making a piece of the old Oban line redundant.

A train arrives from Fort William and links with the train from Oban to make a four-car unit to Glasgow. The train for Fort William arrives; it is busy and there are a lot of hill walkers on it.

Not long after passing Upper Tyndrum, the first station out of Crianlarich, and the scenery is already changing and becoming more majestic with mountains on one side sweeping up into the mist, their sides scored with tracks where water has cascaded down. The line is now following the mountain (Beinn Odhar, 2,948 feet) on one side, across Glen Coralan on a viaduct, and round the side of the next mountain (Beinn Dorain 3,524 feet) via the aptly named Horseshoe Viaduct. The backward view gives you some idea of the challenges that the railway builders had here.

Bridge of Orchy, and the scenery is now becoming more remote. Just beyond the station the road, which had been alongside the railway for some time, now forks off to the left and there is then a sense of isolation heightened by the 3000-foot-plus peaks that loom down on the railway.

Rannoch Moor, and the scenery is now very wild and peaty with heather and miles and miles of undulating mounds and hillocks with lots of wet patches and stagnant peaty pools.

In Rannoch station there is a surprise, as at the other platform is the *Hogwarts Express*, resplendent in its bright red colour. The locomotive is number 5972 and the guard on our train very obligingly allows me some time to run down the platform for a photograph; this is the same friendliness and helpfulness that I experienced last time I travelled with Scotrail.

The next station, Corrour, is even more remote as there isn't even a

The Hogwarts Express

proper road here, and its main purpose seems to be for hill walkers as there are a lot of them getting off, with many of them accompanied by dogs. There is a board that proclaims this place to be 1,347 feet above sea level.

The view after Corrour is high above a valley with Loch Treig at the bottom, and the train then passes through a tunnel and arrives at Tulloch after crossing a viaduct of the same name over the River Spean. There is now a road alongside and the remoteness feel is considerably lessened as we run through Roy Bridge, Spean Bridge and into Fort William.

The changes here have been dramatic since my last visit as all traces of the original station alongside the jetty have vanished completely under a new dual carriageway which enables the road traffic to avoid the town centre. The new station opened in 1975 and is about half a mile further north, nearer to the Mallaig line junction.

There are ten viaducts between Crianlarch and Fort William and the achievement of their construction, like all the rest of the line, is all the more remarkable when you consider the inhospitable environment in which they were constructed.

This journey round Scotland is going to include a ride on the Jacobite steam train to Mallaig but that will be in two days' time and the rest of today will be with Scotrail to Glenfinnan and then back to Oban by road.

Out of the station and across Lochy Viaduct the train slowly approaches the swing bridge over the Caledonian Canal at Banavie; this was completed in 1847 to link Loch Linnhe and Loch Lochy. There are a series of locks here known as Neptune's Staircase and this remarkable engineering feat of eight locks which raised the canal by 64 feet over a 1-mile length was the brainchild of Thomas Telford.

Almost immediately we are passing Corpach station and the area round here is semi-industrial; there is the Arjo Wiggins paper mill and it is good to see that it is still rail connected. The line now follows Loch Eil for about 10 miles and the view across the water is impressive with moorland, forestry and mountains and the wonderfully named Stob Coire a' Chearcaill (2,526 feet).

At a point where the railway is alongside the Callon River we pass through a short tunnel and ahead is Glenfinnan Viaduct; this is probably one of the most famous railway structures in Britain and as the train follows the curve round the River Finnan is 100 feet below. Remarkably, it is built of concrete, surely unusual in railway construction, particularly at the time when it was opened in 1901, but nevertheless today, concrete or not, it blends in with its surroundings and remains a testament to the skill and dedication of the designers and builders. Far below and at the edge of Loch Shiel is the Glenfinnan Monument.

At Glenfinnan station there is a surprise, as waiting in the station is the *Royal Scotsman* diesel locomotive with its rake of vintage maroon coaches.

The *Royal Scotsman*

Glenfinnan station is superbly well preserved and I get into conversation with John Barnes who, as well as running a lovely little railway museum and shop in the station building, is responsible for ensuring the preservation of this time capsule of a country station complete with signal box, a camping coach and two old coaches that are used as a cafe.

From Glenfinnan, the rest of the day will be a leisurely return to Oban by road, but first there is lunch at the nearby Glenfinnan House Hotel set beautifully on the edge of Loch Shiel. As I pass through the front door of this lovely eighteenth-century mansion with its pined panelled walls and roaring log fire, it is like stepping back into another time and a roast beef sandwich and malt whisky for my lunch seems entirely appropriate for the surroundings.

Views from the hotel

The Glenfinnan Monument

Standing on the sweeping lawn in front of the hotel and sipping a 25-year-old malt whisky, I can see the Glenfinnan Monument on the other side of the loch. It was erected in 1815 and was to commemorate the fact that it was on the shores of this loch that Bonnie Prince Charlie landed when he returned to claim the throne that he felt was rightly his. It was also here that he received the allegiance of seven Highland chieftains for a campaign that was to end in disaster at Culloden.

Behind the hotel there are broad-leaved trees in their full autumn splendour, and behind them the green of forestry plantations. This place really has a lovely setting.

There is a brief stop at Banavie to have a close look at the staircase locks and wonder at the magnificent feat of engineering that they represent. The big blocks that form the walls of each lock fit together with Inca-like precision and from where I am standing at the top you cannot help but admire the skill and ingenuity of the man that designed and built this link from the River Lochy to Loch Linnhe.

Driving through Fort William I am impressed not only at the extensiveness of it, but also by the quality of its houses, hotels, transport, shops

The staircase locks looking down

and leisure facilities; some of the villas that front the loch are extremely nice.

The road from Fort William to Oban hugs the shores of Loch Linnhe until we reach Appin, but at Ballachulish there is time to make a small detour and drive through Glen Coe. This is a very atmospheric place and the surrounding mountains stand brooding in the fading sunlight; there is the great Bidean nam Bian (3766 feet) and its outliers, Beinn Fhada, Gear Aonach and Aonach Dubh, also known as the Three Sisters of Glencoe.

Under the orders of William III, on 13th February 1692 Campbell of Glen Lyon and his soldiers massacred the MacDonalds of Glencoe under the order: 'Fall upon the rebels and put all to the sword under seventy'. The reason for this slaughter was that Chief MacIan of Glencoe had been instructed to take the oath of allegiance to the King before 1st January 1692, but when he arrived in Fort William on 31st December 1691 to do this he was then told to go to Inveraray. This delay meant that he did not take the oath until 6th January, with the fateful consequences. Of the 200 inhabitants of the glen, over 40 were slain and the rest fled to the hills where most of them died of exposure, while in the meantime the soldiers burnt down all the hamlets.

A few miles south of Fort William we take a short and unusual refreshment break by making the five-minute ferry crossing from Corran to the pub on the other side at Ardgour, returning by the same route about 30 minutes later.

From Ballachulish, the track bed of the old railway line to Connel can be clearly seen in many places as it sits almost impossibly between the road and the water's edge; it must have been a wonderfully scenic and exciting journey. The only other sign of the railway's existence that I have seen is a caution signal in someone's garden in Ballachulish.

As the road turns inland for a short way just after Portnacroish I can see Castle Stalker perched on a rocky outcrop at the entrance to Loch Laich; it was built by the Stewarts of Appin in 1520 and was used as a hunting lodge by James IV but was then abandoned in 1800. It was later restored in the 1970s by Colonel Stewart Allwood.

There were seven intermediate stations on the Ballachulish to Connel Ferry line before it closed in 1966, and as we cross the river at Connel we are using the original railway bridge which was converted to road use after the line closed. Halfway across there is a plaque that reads: 'Arral's Bridge & Roof Co. 1903'.

Corran from the ferry

Under the bridge at certain times it is possible to see the Falls of Lora, a natural and spectacular phenomenon that is caused by the flow of water between Loch Etive and the Firth of Lorn. When the tidal range of the firth drops below a certain level then the water in the loch rushes out through the narrow gap that is spanned by the bridge. As the tide changes the Atlantic rushes in and causes either a confused mass of water by the bridge, or the falls, depending on the exact state of the tide.

It is only about five or six miles from here to Oban and on the way we pass a restaurant with the interesting name of The Wide Mouthed Frog.

The view from Connel Bridge

The former railway bridge

My first view of Oban from this direction is a good one as rounding a bend in the road you suddenly see the whole town spread out below, and as we pass the brand new Atlantis Leisure Centre with its adjacent bowling green, I decide that I will spend most of tomorrow exploring what seems to me to be an attractive and interesting town.

Strolling down for an early breakfast at 6.45 am, I notice for the first time that a lot of the windows in the hotel have pictures of bygone ferries etched into the glass. Outside it is a glorious sunny day with a clear blue sky and I can see the early morning ferry to Mull gliding across the tranquil waters of the bay. In the harbour there is some activity on the fishing boats.

There are one or two couples strolling along the front but on this early Sunday morning it is still very quiet. I have thought about sitting on the harbour wall in the sunshine and reading the morning paper and watching the swans and ducks that are busy in the shallow water, but there will be time for that later when I have earned it.

McCaig's Tower is opposite and high on the hill, but it is just a short step past the distillery (unfortunately closed today) and across Ardconnel Road to the 144 steps that lead up to it; or so I thought, as at the top there is a steep winding road and I am distinctly warm by the time I have walked up it and reached the tower.

From the outside, the circular two-storey granite building is very like an amphitheatre with apertures right round on each level. The building of it was financed by the merchant banker and philanthropist John Stewart MacCaig, who was inspired by Rome's Coliseum. He employed out-of-work masons to build it and work commenced in 1895; the project cost £5,000. Ambitious plans to add a further storey, a lookout tower, a museum, an art gallery and statues of some of his family members in the windows were abandoned when he died in 1902.

Inside it is very tranquil and restful. The whole area is planted with trees and shrubs and a lawn, and the trees are in their golden and brown autumn colours. A path runs across the middle, and the only sound is that of birds singing.

Outside there is a viewing area that looks across the town and the bay to the Firth of Lorn and the mountains of Mull beyond. These mountains are made of basalt rock spewed out in violent volcanic eruptions 50 million years ago. The grinding action of mighty ice sheets which retreated 10,000 years ago created the rounded shape of many of the islands and mountains. The view from here is something special and makes the climb to get here very worthwhile.

I get into conversation with a man who is making a film of the view.

McCaig's Tower and Oban

From the bottom (and the distillery!)

From the harbour

From the steps halfway up

From the top

From the top

Inside the tower

Inside the tower

On the way down

I am loathe to leave this peaceful spot, and watching Max making his film in a place that he loves, I can't help a slight feeling of envy. It is still quiet, with just the birds singing, and at my feet the hillside drops steeply away and further down I can see the rooftops of some houses peeping through the branches of the trees that cover this hill.

Max says that there is a flying boat day trip service from Glasgow to Oban for part of the year; it is based on demand and it is due to land in the bay at about 2.30 pm, but as it didn't show yesterday there is some doubt about it arriving today. Loch Lomond Seaplanes is based on the Clyde and for about £120 you can enjoy, from the air, the mountains, lochs and castles of this beautiful coastline until the exhilarating splash down in Oban Bay.

Back down at sea level, and wandering around the North Pier I come across the Argyle Hotel, a large building with towers and pinnacles which in its day must have been an impressive and desirable place to stay; unfortunately it is now boarded up and is a very sad sight. A bit further on by Corran Esplanade is the Oban Inn, dating from 1790.

At the other end of town and almost hidden away is a Tesco, which is very handy for a cup of coffee and a sandwich. To get here I have walked the entire length of George Street with its very tall and slightly forbidding architecture and towards the end there are some eating establishments with names like McTavish's Kitchen and the Spinnaker Café; there are also popular high street shops but I am reminded that the girl I spoke to on the boat said that there was not much choice of clothes for people of her age. As I am thinking that I come across a shop selling young girls' clothes and there is a tee shirt in the window with emblazoned on the front the words: 'Buy it now, tell mum later'.

After my exertions and the sandwich I feel that I have done enough for today and head for the harbour. Basking in the beautiful sunshine on a bench on the harbour front I feel totally relaxed. There are lots of people about now and it is obviously a very popular spot to come to on a sunny Sunday; some are just sitting reading papers, while others stroll up and down. A group of motorcyclists have just arrived but the noise of their arrival is short-lived as they have peeled off their helmets and are now chatting amongst themselves. All the bikes are spotlessly clean and there are a couple of Harley Davidsons with their chrome shining in the sun. The water is lapping at the bottom of the sea wall, the flower beds are a blaze of red begonias, the sun is warm, there is no litter, people are chatting happily and the two swans that I saw this morning are busy preening themselves; it is indeed a nice place to be.

A girl on the boat described Oban as a bit Gothic and medieval but to my mind this was a bit harsh, as although some of the architecture is heavily Victorian, the place does have charm and interest and the impression that I get is of a town that is comfortable with itself.

After a relaxing day in Oban, it is an early start the following day for the hour's drive to Fort William. There, I find myself standing on the platform of the station, basking in the sight, sound and smell of the locomotive that, with its rake of maroon period carriages, is going to take me to Mallaig. It is Black Five 45407 and is immaculately turned out.

The Black Five at Fort William

Any chance of me driving it?

Almost from the off I am leaning out of the window enjoying everything about this ride. The backdrop of wonderful scenery complements the sounds and feel of this journey, the beat of the locomotive, the swaying of the carriages, the 'clickerty clack, clickerty clack' of the wheels on jointed rails, the smell of the smoke, even the coal dust in the eye: the whole experience takes me back to my days on the railway when these locomotives were a common sight. I have a great feeling of nostalgia or, as the Oxford dictionary puts it, 'wistful memory of an earlier time' or 'sentimental yearning for a period of the past'.

The view from Loch Eil Outward Bound station

We will soon be at Glenfinnan station and at this point between Locheilside and Glenfinnan the gradient of the line increases and the locomotive is working hard and leaving a long plume of smoke behind us, I have the sound at this point on tape but it is very hard to reproduce in words and the nearest that I can come to it is a rapid 'chutterter chutterter chutterter'.

Glenfinnan Viaduct

138

Flora MacDonald   Steaming hot tea

The line is now curving slightly away and from the left I get a broadside view of Glenfinnan Viaduct as its 21 arches march across the valley.

Glenfinnan station, and to greet us at the station is a young woman in full highland costume, complete with bagpipes. Her name is Flora MacDonald. She is from Fort William and is playing with a lot of enthusiasm. When I ask her afterwards what she was playing she tells me that it was 'Scotland the Brave' and 'Itchy Fingers'. It was very enjoyable, but then I do enjoy listening to the pipes.

From here the line twists and turns along the shores of Loch Eilt with the wheels squealing, and as we cross Loch nan Uamh Viaduct we are high above a lovely beach; this is the Atlantic Ocean.

Loch Eilt   Back the way we came

Arisaig: this is the most westerly station in Britain. Between here and Lochailort I counted eight tunnels and three viaducts all of which are a testament to the skill and determination of the men that built this line.

Mallaig station is a bit of a shock for me, as the last time I was here there was a locomotive shed, a turntable and several sidings. All that appears to have disappeared, but it was a long time ago. There is just one

Arisaig station

The view from Morar Viaduct

main line into the station and two on the other side which appear to be little used.

There is a plaque in the station that reads: 'This plaque was unveiled by the Hon. Sir William McAlpine on 10th May 2001 to commemorate the centenary of the Mallaig extension of the West Highland Railway, opened on the first of April 1901'.

I get into conversation with the driver and he invites me onto the footplate and shows me all the controls; it is a wonderful feeling as I have never before stood on the footplate of a Black Five in front of its open fire box.

Outside nothing much seems to have changed over the years in this little fishing port except for a couple of new shops and cafes; the cafes are doing very brisk business from the train passengers. After a stroll round it is time to head for the ferry as the rest of the day is a tour round Skye before heading for my hotel in Kyle of Lochalsh.

On board the ferry, *Coruisk*, it is very clear and the mountains of Skye ahead are very impressive; some of them have sunlight slanting across them

Fish train at Mallaig, July 1964

Mallaig from the ferry

while others stand out starkly against a grey sky. The ferry docks at Armadale and here is the Clan Donald Centre and Castle Gardens.

The Macdonalds arrived on Skye in the fifteenth century and had a powerful influence on Scottish history and held extensive estates from Ulster to Skye; they were also Lords of the Isles until the Scottish King took the title away in 1493. Gradually the lands of the Clan Donald were sold until only the land at Armadale remained and when this came up for sale in 1971 it was bought by the Clan Donald Lands Trust who are the custodians of this 20,000-acre estate. Flora MacDonald was married at Armadale in November 1750 and in 1790 Lord MacDonald built a new mansion house. This was extended in 1815 and became Armadale Castle although much of it was subsequently destroyed by fire in1855. There are magnificent gardens to walk round, and thanks to the Gulf Stream and the usually frost-free atmosphere, exotic trees, shrubs and flowers thrive here and it is a very pleasant place to take a stroll.

From here we are going to backtrack a little and head for Sligachan, but first there is a short stop at Isleornsay to try samples from the Gaelic Whisky collection. The company that produces these fine whiskies is Praban na Linne and was set up in 1976 by Sir Iain Noble of Eilean Iarmain to supply the Gaelic-speaking islands of the north-west coast of Scotland. This small privately owned company is in an idyllic spot. There is a grassed area outside leading to a small private harbour, and just across the water is the island of Ornsay from which this place takes its name. The sun is shining and reflecting off the white painted lighthouse on Ornsay and beyond that, across the Sound of Sleat, are the majestic mountains of the mainland.

There is a lovely whitewashed hotel and a building dating from 1812 from where the whisky is produced. Inside that little building I am invited

The view from Isleornsay

to sample different whiskies, all with very Gaelic and interesting-looking names. My favourite whiskey (note the spelling!) is Jameson, but I thought it best not to mention that here in this haven of home-produced Scottish malts.

From here we have joined the main road from Kyle and are passing through Broadford. The road is now running alongside the water with the island of Scalpay just offshore; on the other side I can see the dark peak of a mountain with a skirt of cloud all around its base.

A bit further on and we are passing through a place called Luib, a tiny hamlet on the banks of an inlet of the Sound of Raasay. This and the surrounding area has a very remote feel to it. The road follows this inlet round and high up on the far side, looking like a toy, is a large lorry struggling up the hill. From this distance you can't tell that it is a road as it looks more like a line drawn on the mountainside.

The weather is clearing and from the base of the inlet we are now climbing into the heart of very mountainous country; the mountains look very tall, very forbidding and very permanent. There is a lovely cascade of water pouring down through a gap in the mountains: it crashes and tumbles over rocks at the bottom and then flows quietly across the road and into the loch.

We have dropped down to the head of Loch Sligachan and across a small bridge and are making a short stop for a coffee at the Sligachan Hotel. As far as I can see there is no other habitation in sight but this place is popular with hill walkers as well as passers-by like myself.

The original inn was about half a mile nearer the head of the loch by a natural ford, the name Sligachan translated from the Gaelic being 'small shells' and the spot became known as the 'shelly place'. The original inn was relocated to its present position in 1830, and sitting between the loch

The old bridge at Sligachan

and the Cuillin Hills it is a very attractive, but remote-looking spot. The Cuillin Hills form a ridge about seven miles long with rocky and jagged peaks; the highest point on the island of Skye is Black Cuillin at 3,255 feet. Just by the car park there is display board showing the names and heights of the individual hills of the Cuillins,

Inside the hotel there are some interesting reminders of its past that include photographs of licensees in the nineteenth century such as Mrs Sharp, lessee of Sligachan Inn from 1895. She is an attractive woman wearing the high-necked dress of the day. There is a list of the owners and tenants of the inn from 1841 onwards and also a copy of the Innkeepers Liability Act 1863 (an Act to amend the law in respect of liability of innkeepers and to prevent certain frauds upon them). It was 1 shilling (5p) on publication. There is a picture of Norman Magnus Macleod of Macleod, the 26th Chief (1839–1929). He stands proudly in full Highland regalia and with, somewhat incongruously, a flat hat.

After a swift coffee and biscuit we are on our way to Portree. This turns out to be an attractive little town with a population of about 2,500 and at this point we are more than 200 miles from Glasgow.

There is a central square with locals and tourists sitting around either just talking or poring over maps. The small bus station in the middle is quite busy as are the surrounding shops: it is, of course, the capital of Skye.

Strolling down Wentworth Street I have found an interesting shop, and although it seems to sell mainly tourist things there are also some very nice other items as well and I spend some time in here, and money as well! A little way in Bank Street is the Tourist Information Centre and this has a comprehensive range of information and items for sale, as well as being the place where you can book travel tickets.

All this walking has given me an appetite and I am recommended to

Outside the tourist information shop

try the fish and chip shop on the harbour front. From Bank Street this is reached by an extremely steep flight of steps, but at the bottom is a delightful little harbour and, without any disrespect to Portree, it could have come straight out of Cornwall. There is a little pier at the end and there are fishing boats tied up at the quayside. Strolling past the little pier I see a headland of open ground known as The Lump, although I wasn't able to find out why. The fish and chips are as excellent as promised and probably the best that I have had; the seagulls certainly think so as well.

Portree harbour

Portree has been a very nice place to visit and despite being the capital there is a definite sense of a slower pace of life here. I feel a bit sad to leave, but there is one more place to see today before I head for the Kyle of Lochalsh and my hotel for the night.

North-West, and we are running along the bottom of Loch Snizort where the sea is very blue. The road now leaves the loch side and we are in area of heathland and heather before we pass through the picturesque little village of Dunvegan and reach the castle of the same name. There is a meandering drive lined with rhododendrons and azaleas and then suddenly

Dunvegan Castle

there is the main door set in this massive four-square towered castle, the seat of the Macleod chiefs who have occupied it for more than seven centuries.

Inside it is very warm and everything breathes history with family portraits of long-ago chiefs and their wives, swords and armour, ancient tapestries, four-poster beds, polished wood floors, even stairs to the fifteenth-century dungeon. In a very small room inside the walls there is an iron grill set in the middle of the floor and 20 feet below is a mock-up of a tiny dungeon, complete with dummy and realistic sound effects.

As I wander from room to room, if it wasn't for the warmth and the electric light it could almost be from any period of the castle's history. I have found a lovely old grandfather clock and can't resist opening the door to see if it is an eight-day or 30-hour movement; the door won't shut and keeps swinging open! I start to get warm as I know that I should probably not have touched it but still walk back down the long corridor to confess all to the impassive-looking attendant sitting on a small chair. I start to babble some sort of defence but he just says that the door should have

The dining room at Dunvegan

been locked anyway and we then get into a friendly conversation about clocks, his job and where he lives. Not surprisingly he is local and loves his job and I must say that there are worse things in life than supervising a warm and historic castle.

One of the rooms has a treasure trove of artefacts which include a lock of hair clipped from the head of Bonnie Prince Charlie by Flora MacDonald as a keepsake and preserved in a locket, together with Bonnie Prince Charlie's waistcoat; there is also a pair of glasses belonging to Donald MacLeod, the boatman who helped Bonnie Prince Charlie on his sea crossings, and a pincushion belonging to Flora MacDonald with the names of some of those who suffered in the 1745 rebellion embroidered on it.

Outside, the castle stands on a high crag above the loch and commands a view of all the entrances in what would have been a very strategic position. Within the battlements there are still some cannons, reminders of an age when the castle faced very different challenges.

The view from the high battlements up Loch Dunvegan is quite spectacular and the white sail of a tiny yacht is set against the vivid blue of the sea and the golds and browns and greens of the trees on each side; it is a view that has probably not changed for hundreds of years.

We are now on the way to Kyle and are passing Bracadale on the west coast of Skye. From here I can now see the other side of the Cullins and their sheer slopes. Most of them have their tops wreathed in cloud and there is a very interesting light as we near the end of the day as it is a mixture of dark grey, light grey, streaks of sunlight and some blue sky.

Not long after Sligachan we have entered a glen and have to pull over to let two lorries past; each one is carrying a single blade for an offshore wind turbine and close up they are really huge.

After a long day it is good to cross the Skye Bridge and check in at the comfortable Kyle hotel – which is 585 miles from London. After a very pleasant dinner I head for my room and an early night.

First thing today is an enjoyable boat trip around the Kyle in a glass-bottomed boat and while there is very little to see underwater there are some otters and several colonies of seals on the little seaweed-covered rocks. It is also a nice way to view the Skye Bridge at close quarters as it is an interesting construction in that it appears to be a different shape depending from what angle you are looking: from the boat on the seaward side it appears banana-shaped, while from another angle it seems more like a horseshoe. Since my last trip to Scotland and the election of the SNP (Scottish National Party) to government, the toll charges on the Skye Bridge have been abolished.

Eilean Ban – Kyle   Wind turbine blades – Kyle

There are four small islands just off the quay at Kyle which are home
to several types of seabird; one of the islands, known as the Black Isle, has
a colony of shags. The four islands were bought by a man at an auction
in Birmingham; he didn't want them but didn't want anything to happen
to them, so after his purchase he gave the islands to the RSPB.

Although the station at Kyle of Lochalsh is currently manned there are
no trains, as due to a landslip near Duncraig they are currently terminating
and starting from Strathcarron. The repair work is now complete but
normal service will not resume for another three days, by which time I
will have moved on to Inverness. This change to the train journey gives
the opportunity to make a detour along the shores of Loch Alsh to visit
Eilean Donan Castle and then drive on to Strathcarron.

The brochure describes Eilean Donan Castle as Scotland's most romantic
castle and it has certainly appeared on many calendars and jigsaws as well
as being photographed on countless occasions. It stands on a small rocky
island that is joined to the mainland by a narrow stone bridge and its
setting between the waters of Loch Duich and the mountains behind is
certainly something special.

The original medieval castle was built in the thirteenth century and was
the stronghold of the Mackenzies of Kintail until it was reduced to a ruin
in 1719 when it was garrisoned by Spanish troops and Jacobite sympathisers
who were attacked and bombarded by three men o' war of the English
Navy. After that, the castle lay in ruins for the next 200 years until in
1912 a restoration programme started which was completed in 1932.

The Great Hall is beautiful with its huge paintings of ancestors along
each side and the huge fireplace with tiles that depict Highland chieftains
of long ago. The oak-beamed ceiling, polished wooden floors and huge
oak dining table all combine to make this hall a very special-looking place;
there is even a short staircase up to a little balcony where you can look

Eilean Donan Castle

down on proceedings and it would make a wonderful photograph, but unfortunately that is strictly forbidden and monitored.

The castle is now home to the Clan Macrae and the name of the present incumbent is Marigold; she is 78 years old and has five daughters and 20 grandchildren.

There is a long winding stone staircase up to the next floor where there are some delightful bedrooms with little alcoves and windows looking out on the loch. Back in the Great Hall there is a good-natured argument about the age of one of the many grandfather clocks. A particular one has caught my eye as it is beautifully polished and has a galleon rocking on waves as its second hand. The maker is G. Foster of Sittingbourne and the lady attendants here have told me that it is dated 1815, but the attendant upstairs says that it is 1810; either way it is from the era of the battle of Waterloo and still going strong.

It is time to go as there is a train to catch at Strathcarron. The road back from Auchtertyre climbs steeply into the mountains with a rather grim view of dying ferns, heather and black rocks, but looking back into

Over the hills from Auchtertyre

the distance I can see the Five Sisters of Kintail. They are a dramatic range of mountains that rise from the head of Loch Duich to heights of over 3,000 feet and are said to be the steepest grass-sloped mountains in Scotland.

We have reached Stromeferry and from here the road follows the railway, side by side along the shores of Loch Carron, until it climbs again and we are in the middle of forestry high above the line, and then down to loch level as we pass Attdale station, which is really just a halt for Attadale Gardens.

Strathcarron is a nice little wayside hamlet set in a valley and surrounded by mountains. There is a lovely row of little black and white cottages and the Strathcarron Hotel, with a sign above the hotel door that says: 'Warning, this hotel may contain nuts'. After a warming bowl of soup it is time to go, and the two-car unit for Inverness is patiently waiting. Strathcarron is one of the very few stations on this line that still has a passing loop, and is the obvious choice for this temporary terminus.

This part of my Scottish journey to Inverness is covered by my earlier trip so I will only mention things that are different this time, the main one being the weather, as this time the sun is shining and last time there was snow everywhere and quite deep in places; surprisingly, both trips were taken at the same time of year.

We have just passed a lovely little sandstone cottage covered in ivy and bright red leaves; it turns out to be the station house at Achnashellach. There are beautiful autumn colours around the station and signs that it was once double tracked here, as I suspect most of the stations were.

Just nearing Achnasheen, and a Tornado aircraft comes screaming down the valley. It is no height at all from the ground and seems an intrusion in this pretty little hamlet by the river, where the station has a little cafe.

Between Achanalt and Garve the line sweeps in a graceful curve around Loch Luichart and the autumn colours here are at their splendid best. Garve station seems to end the remoteness of this journey as there are big houses with manicured lawns and an attractive terrace of pink-coloured houses. There are two platforms at Garve and the station building is painted in a brilliant mustard colour; setting it off is a brilliant red rowan tree. Just after Garve is the loch of the same name and I mention it because the water is absolutely motionless and it is like a giant mirror: it can't be like that very often I would have thought. Not long after and we are perched high on the side of a hill looking across a beautiful green open valley with tree-covered mountains in the background.

Inverness: it is a glorious sunny day and the town is still the same attractive, busy and lots-to-do place that I remember from four years ago; a lot of new shops have also been built.

I have a couple of hours to spare before moving to Aviemore via Carrbridge and must first look up Sheila from the bookshop on the station before I go. It is lovely to meet up again after so long a time and in-between customers we talk railways, work, travel, health and the fact that we have both acquired grandchildren since we last met.

Time for coffee in the Pumpkin Cafe and here I get into conversation with Zuana who is from Slovakia. She has been here for only two weeks but her family have been here a lot longer. Her English is very good and she says that Scotland is beautiful but her country is beautiful as well but that she has come here for a better life and more money.

There is now just time to have a look at the river and watch the water bubbling over the shallows, explore a couple of bookshops, buy a memory card for my digital camera and it is time to go. Inverness is one of my favourite places and it will be nice to come again.

Leaving Inverness on what looks like a new dual carriageway, there is a great sweeping vista of fields and trees and we are closely following the railway which is the express line from Inverness to Perth. At Tomatin there is the magnificent Findhorn Viaduct where the railway crosses the river of the same name. The steel trusses of this bridge are supported on masonry

Inverness Victorian Market

Bridge over the River Ness

Church in Inverness

Nice architecture – Inverness

Inverness station

piers and it curves gracefully as it crosses the river; the whole structure blends superbly with its surroundings.

We are only going to make a short stop at Carrbridge in order to have a look at the interesting old pack horse bridge over the river; it is the oldest stone bridge in the Highlands. It is indeed a very interesting bridge, not to say precarious, as it is extremely narrow and I cannot imagine a pack

The Findhorn Viaduct

horse picking its way over the rough surface without falling into the tumbling waters below. There is a plaque with the following information:

At the beginning of the eighteenth century to the inconvenience of both travellers and local people there was no point at which the River Dulnain could be crossed when it was in spate and burials in the church at Duthil were often delayed. Brigadier General Alexander Grant, Grant Clan Chief, commissioned John Niccelsone, a mason from Ballindalloch to build a bridge at Dalrachney in 1717. The bridge was paid for out of stipends of the parish of Duthil. Its parapets and side rules were badly damaged in the eighteenth century and again in the famous flood of August 1829 giving the appearance that it still has today.

I get into conversation with the local garage owner whose premises adjoin the river, and he tells me about another well-known flood in November 1978. He has photographs, and the sight of the surging, raging torrent that passed under the bridge must have been quite frightening.

The River Dulnain, 2007   The River Dulnain, 1978

Nearby are the ruins of Inverlaidan House where Bonnie Prince Charlie stayed on the eve of the rout of Moy in 1746.

Aviemore is a bustling tourist town, mainly along the one main street, and my hotel is a modern and comfortable affair opposite the railway station. The view from my window is of the Cairngorms but it is getting a bit dark now to take a photograph.

Breakfast, and my first opportunity on this journey to have my favourite breakfast, which is strong coffee, buttered toast and fried egg on a plate of haggis. Delicious.

This morning is a double journey on the Strathspey Steam Railway which runs from Aviemore to Broomhill, with the station of Boat of Garten in-between. Before we set off I stroll down to Aviemore station for a look round. It is an attractive place, having been restored to its Victorian glory, and it really looks nice. In the booking office I get into conversation with Alan. He says that railways are on the up in Scotland and there is a tremendous amount of traffic now with so many people moving out of the city to live and then travelling in; he says that the roads are horrendous and more and more people are turning to the trains. He enjoys his job as a booking clerk very much and says that a job on the railway in Scotland is very secure now due to greatly increased passenger numbers – great to hear. He relates how a conductor colleague of his on the Aberdeen train the other day took over £1,000 on one journey and that was just for people who did not have ticket; places like Elgin and Nairn are now very busy.

A short drive takes us to Boat of Garten (so called because there used to be a ferry here a long time ago) station which is very impressive and beautifully maintained. The station building is in clean white and brown paint and several colourful flower baskets are hanging; it has its original station clock and there are also several old tin plate advertising signs for things like soap. The stationmaster is in attendance and in full uniform.

Sitting at the platform is a little Barclays tank engine. She is painted green with her name, *Braeriach* (the name of the second-highest mountain in the Cairngorms) on the side in yellow, and behind her are six vintage maroon carriages.

We are under way to Aviemore and the little tank is making a superb job of pulling the six carriages, but it is helped by the fact that this line runs through a valley and is more or less level for most of its way. The 'chuff, chuff' of the locomotive, the plume of smoke and the steam coming up from the joint between the carriages are all very evocative and enjoyable.

There are a few minutes in Aviemore before we head back, this time to the present terminus at Broomhill, and I stroll down to talk with the driver and breathe in the aroma of the locomotive. On the side of the cab there is a plate that says: 'Andrew Barclay Sons and Co. Ltd. Caledonia Works No. 2017 1935 Kilmarnock'. There is another plate that indicates that her Strathspey number is 17.

Back in Boat of Garten and there are a lot coaches and tankers in the sidings and an old DMU as well, 'old' being the operative word. Remarkably, it is in faded pink and yellow. There is also an old Bo Bo locomotive. There is a train in the other platform pulled by locomotive number D5862: it is the *Royal Scotsman* that we saw a few days ago in Glenfinnan.

Aviemore station (Strathspey side)

Braeriach at Aviemore

Boat of Garten station

On the way to Broomhill there are hundreds and hundreds of sections of sleepered rails at the trackside. When I ask the guard about them he says that they were donated and will be used to relay the track between Broomhill and Grantown-on-Spey over the coming winter months.

Approaching Broomhill station

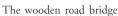
The wooden road bridge   View from the bridge

The line runs through a very fertile valley with green fields and grazing cows; not far away the River Spey flows placidly along. There is not a lot at Broomhill, just the little station building and a platform in the middle of nowhere, albeit a very pleasant nowhere. A few hundred yards away there is an old bridge across the Spey, and crossing this ancient wooden structure I find a plaque on the other side that shows it was erected in 1894.

The Strathspey Railway has been a nice experience and I am looking forward to the Keith & Dufftown Railway later today, but first there is a visit to the site of the last battle to take place on British mainland soil at Culloden when the forces of King George II under the command of the Duke of Cumberland defeated the Jacobite forces of Bonnie Prince Charlie.

Talking to the receptionist at the Culloden Visitor Centre, who is obviously not from this part of the world, she says that she came here from her native Cheshire for a holiday, met a Scotsman, married him, acquired the surname of MacDonald and stayed. She loves it here. Inside there is a film presentation of the events of April 1746 and a series of drawings and pictures relating to stages of the battle.

Plan of Culloden Battlefield

155

Outside the centre is a large windswept moor with a track across the middle, and after a few yards I am looking at the Well of the Dead. It is a pear-shaped stone by the side of a small well and is the spot where the body was found of Alexander MacGillivray of Dunmaglass, who led his men of Clan Chattan in a charge that broke through the first line of defence of Cumberland's men before he was killed.

Just a few steps away are more stones marking the graves where the members of different clans were buried: Cameron, Chattan, Stewart of Appin, Grant, Macleod, Fraser and others. Beyond these graves on a spot halfway between the opposing armies is a stone cairn that was erected in 1881 as a memorial. The plaque on it reads:

THE BATTLE OF CULLODEN was fought on this moor 16 April 1746 The Graves of the Gallant Highlanders who fought for SCOTLAND AND PRINCE CHARLIE are marked by the names of their clans.

The stone cairn

Lord George Murray was the outstanding field commander for the Prince, but his advice was not heeded by the Prince who depended on John William O'Sullivan, adjutant to the Army and an Irish soldier of fortune. In the end O'Sullivan was responsible for much of the failure of the campaign, and his disastrous choice of battleground may have been decisive, as the wide bare moor was ideal for Cumberland's cavalry and his disciplined infantry. The battle lasted less than an hour and the rout was complete.

The aftermath of the battle was terrible, as Cumberland had previously captured and issued a copy of the Prince's battle orders to his troops but with a forged addition saying that no quarter was to be given. The effect of this was that the government troops, after the battle, slaughtered indiscriminately not only the fleeing clansmen, but also innocent bystanders including women and children. This was followed by a systematic process of murder and mutilation which, according to a poster in the Culloden Visitor Centre, an English historian described as 'such as never perhaps before or since disgraced a British army.' I found the exhibition in the visitor centre and the walk round the battlefield both fascinating and very moving.

We are on the last journey of the day and meeting us off the Inverness train at Keith Station, which is now a small modern affair, is a local coach driver who is taking us to Dufftown.

We have just passed Strathisla Distillery which was founded in 1786, it is the oldest working distillery in Scotland and produces Chivas Regal Strathisla malt.

At Dufftown station I am greeted by Rod, the driver of DMU 73119 that will take us on the journey to the station at Keith Town and back.

Strathisla Distillery

We are instantly into nostalgic talk, mostly from me, as the sight and sounds of the DMU have taken me straight back to the 1960s when I worked on a line where these were introduced alongside steam. He tells me that the line was closed by British Railways in 1991 but fortunately the track was not lifted, and after years of refurbishment it reopened to passengers in 2000.

Close by is the world-famous Glenfiddich Distillery, opened by William Grant in 1879.

Shortly after leaving the station the line curves round on a very high viaduct over the River Fiddich and I can look down on many warehouses full of casks of malt whisky. The line now starts to climb a little and we are in an area of forest and through the trees I can see a loch. There is a charming little incident as the train slows down to let a little deer get out of the way. As I stand swaying in the guard's van I am drinking Glenfiddich: the swaying is because of the motion of the train.

We have slowed down again, this time for a pony that is munching at the line side by a delightful little bridge. Just before we enter the little station at Keith Town we pass Strathisla distillery. It still has its rail connection, although it is no longer used.

Rodd the driver

The viaduct at Dufftown

The journey back to Dufftown is the same and just as delightful. We even meet the deer again! The whole trip has been a delightful ramble through some very serene and attractive countryside with pine forests, beautiful woodlands and rolling green fields.

There is a long drive back to Aviemore and on the way we pass the Glenlivet Distillery which seems to be in the middle of nowhere. It is a beautiful sunset tonight and the sun goes down behind the mountains in a blaze of orange that slowly turns to pale blue and then the dark blue of night.

On the way back to Dufftown

Dufftown Station

After a couple of malts and a leisurely dinner I am ready for bed and the train home in the morning. Standing in the booking hall at Aviemore the following morning with half an hour before my train is due I get into conversation with Willy, who has been with the railway 47 years and started at what was then Keith Junction; he now lives in Aviemore. We chatted for quite a while and shared reminiscences about the 1960s when we were both working on what was a very different railway; we both agreed that there had been a 'family feeling' about the job, particularly when you met other railmen.

Des – a happy Scotsman

He says that platform 3 at Aviemore was originally the platform for trains that went to Forres and the platforms and old derelict station with the name board 'Aviemore Strathspey' about half a mile north of here (and through which the current Strathspey trains now run) was the original station for the Strathspey Railway which ran from Aviemore to Craigellachie on the Keith to Elgin line.

As I settle into my seat for the journey to Glasgow I reflect on my journeys around Scotland. They have both been extremely enjoyable and I have seen and done many new things, I have also seen and done things that I have done before, but somehow they seemed new all over again.

Scotland is like that, as it gives the impression of never changing, whereas in fact, it is always changing and offering you some new sight or experience and it is a place that I look forward to visiting again in the not too distant future.